The Illogic of
American Nuclear Strategy

CORNELL STUDIES IN
SECURITY AFFAIRS

edited by Robert J. Art
and Robert Jervis

The Illogic of American Nuclear Strategy

ROBERT JERVIS

Cornell University Press

ITHACA AND LONDON

*This book was written under the auspices of the
Institute of War and Peace Studies and the Research
Institute on International Change, Columbia University.*

First published 1984 by Cornell University.
Published in the United Kingdom by
Cornell University Press Ltd., London.

International Standard Book Number 0–8014–1715–5
Library of Congress Catalog Card Number 84–7731
Printed in the United States of America
*Librarians: Library of Congress cataloging information
appears on the last page of the book.*

*The paper in this book is acid-free and meets the guidelines for permanence
and durability of the Committee on Production Guidelines for
Book Longevity of the Council on Library Resources.*

*To James King, Thomas Schelling, Glenn Snyder,
and the memory of Bernard Brodie, who developed
so many of the ideas I have used.*

Contents

Contents

Acknowledgments

I am grateful to the several friends and colleagues who commented on earlier drafts of this book: Godfried van den Bergh, Ole Holsti, Zalmay Khalilzad, Gert Krell, Benjamin Lambeth, Joshua Lederberg, Richard Ned Lebow, David MacIsaac, Jeffrey Richelson, Dennis Ross, Glenn Snyder, and Jack Snyder. Robert Art, Richard Betts, and Richard Ullman provided more help than any author has the right to expect, going through multiple drafts with enormous care and insight. Also beyond the call of duty were the efforts of Walter Lippincott in urging me to turn a preliminary paper into a book and Kay Scheuer in removing many infelicities of expression.

Columbia University's Institute of War and Peace Studies and Research Institute on International Change provided exciting homes in which to work, and the completion of this book was assisted by grants from the Ford Foundation to these institutes. The work also benefited from comments made at the conference "Deterrence, Strategy, and Psychology" sponsored by the Rockefeller Foundation in May 1983.

R. J.

Everything about the atomic bomb is overshadowed by the twin facts that it exists and that its destructive power is fantastically great.

—Bernard Brodie, *The Absolute Weapon* (1946)

Senator Glenn. I get lost in what is credible and not credible. This whole thing gets so incredible when you consider wiping out whole nations, it is difficult to establish credibility.

Secretary Brown. That is why we sound a little crazy when we talk about it.

—U.S. Senate, Committee on Foreign Relations,
Hearing on Presidential Directive 59,
September 16, 1980

Preface

Nuclear strategy is often seen as an arcane subject—and in detail it is. But one need not be an expert to understand the crucial issues. Indeed, expert discussion, which often revolves around the characteristics of specific weapons or the comparison of various arms-control proposals, frequently glosses over the fundamental questions on which analysis must rest. How one answers these questions in large part determines the stance one takes on a wide range of separate issues. We need to ask ourselves how nuclear weapons have altered world politics and, more particularly, how the fact that both superpowers are vulnerable to destruction affects the ways force and the threat of force can be used to reach foreign-policy goals.

American nuclear strategy for the past decade—the "countervailing strategy"—has been based on the assumption that what is crucial today, as it was in the past, is the ability of American and allied military forces to deny the Soviets a military advantage from any aggression they might contemplate. The United States must be prepared to meet and block Soviet force at any level of violence. The strategy, then, is generally one of counterforce: blocking and seeking to destroy Soviet military power. Its goal is deterrence. Although it is concerned with how the United States would fight many different kinds of wars, both nuclear and nonnuclear, one cannot correctly claim that the strategy is designed with the intent to engage in wars rather then to deter them. In fact, its advocates argue that the best way

[11]

to deter wars and aggression is to be prepared to fight if need be: the Russians are unlikely to start or risk a war if they know they will be defeated. The main theme of this book is that this argument, which makes perfect sense in a nonnuclear world, is profoundly misleading in the current era of abundant weapons of mass destruction. To a significant extent, current strategy fits with common sense; but nuclear weapons do not.

Because nuclear weapons enable the state that is losing a war to destroy the other side, they have produced a true revolution in strategy. In the past, military advantage allowed a state both to harm the other and to protect itself. Now protection is possible only with the other's cooperation. As I will try to show throughout this book, the result is that the current stress on being able to contain Soviet military thrusts at all levels of violence is misguided. Such planning makes a great deal of sense in terms of traditional military thought—a country can deter an adversary by being able to deny it the ability to reach its expansionist goals. But mutual vulnerability means that what now deters is the fear of the overwhelming costs of engaging in large-scale violence.

All-out war is obviously suicidal. Everyone recognizes this, but some go on to claim that this very fact means that nuclear weapons have very little influence, that the only thing the threat of all-out war can deter is a massive strike by the other side. If the Russians were able to win a military adventure at a lower level of violence, for example by a conventional war in Europe, they might launch such an attack, confident that their nuclear forces would deter the use of ours. Many of those who reject the countervailing strategy agree that nuclear stalemate increases the chance of nonnuclear conflict. Thus Robert McNamara argues that the "sole purpose" of strategic nuclear forces "is to deter the other side's first use of its strategic forces" and calls for the West to build up its conventional forces to a level at which they could repel a conventional Soviet attack.[1] But those who hold such views fail to appreciate the fact that statesmen, both Soviet and American, cannot know that violence will not spread. Using military force is terribly risky. History is filled with cases in which small wars escalated, either because of accidents or because of explicit decisions. Without denying the irrationality of a major nuclear response to limited aggression, I will argue that because force cannot be easily controlled or compartmentalized, the fear of nuclear war does deter the other side from much more than nuclear attack. Irrational as it may be, the chance of devastation has made our world unusually safe.

As long as the societies of both sides are vulnerable (and few except President Reagan believe that missile defenses will ever be able to protect cites), gaining military advantage or denying it to the other side is much less important than the risks states are willing to run to further their values. Threats and force thus work differently from the way they did in the past. Because the countervailing strategy fails to take this into account, it cannot be accepted. The proponents of the doctrine of course realize that nuclear weapons have made some changes in world politics and know that each side can destroy the other. But because these insights are at variance with the ideas that provide the foundations of the strategy, when those ideas are worked out in detail they present a maze of incoherence and contradictions. To show this requires examining the strategy at length, and I have done so in chapters 3 and 4. These portions of the book, especially chapter 4, necessarily contain somewhat technical arguments, and nonspecialists may wish to skip them.

Overall, however, this book is designed for both experts and concerned citizens. In chapter 1, I argue that the changes nuclear weapons have produced in world politics constitute a true revolution in the relationships between force and foreign policy. The fact that neither side can protect itself without the other's cooperation drastically alters the way in which force can be used or threatened. The impulses toward both cooperation and conflict are increased, and statesmen understandably seek ways out of the resulting dilemmas. As chapter 2 shows, nuclear weapons inevitably bring with them new and painful tensions for policy. All too often the reaction has been to try to find ways of escape which, while psychologically attractive, cannot work because they do not come to grips with the implications of the nuclear revolution. The most important of these for current policy is "conventionalization"—the attempt to understand our world by employing the intellectual tools of the prenuclear era. One result of this way of thinking is the countervailing strategy. It is described in the third chapter, and its crucial terms and assertions are examined to show how the faulty starting point inevitably leads to incoherence. In the next chapter specific issues are analyzed to show the precise ways in which the strategy contradicts itself. These detailed problems are part of the broader issue treated in chapter 5: whether the United States can deter attacks against which it lacks adequate defenses. I argue that it can, because in the nuclear era what matters most to statesmen is not who would win a local and isolated military encounter between the superpowers, but the risk that a conflict would lead to all-out war. In concluding, I discuss what my position implies for the design of a more sensible policy.

Criticizing a strategy is easier than designing an appropriate one, and I have been able to take only a few tentative steps in that direction. An adequate policy must start from an appreciation of the nuclear revolution, of the ways in which mutual vulnerability has altered the traditional relationships between force and foreign policy. Although of course we want to reduce the risk of war as much as possible, it is the chance of war—however small—that deters forcible alterations of the political status quo. I believe that each side's awareness of the utter destructiveness of large-scale nuclear war means that the chances of war between the United States and the USSR are very slight—even if the United States continues to follow its foolish policy—and that the Russians can be deterred from major military adventures. Our security problems are less severe than we usually think. This does not mean that dangers are absent, however. Most dangerous is a situation which current policy neglects: if either side came to believe that war was inev-

itable, deterrence could not work. That is, deterrence is prem-
ised on convincing the other side not only that awful things will
happen if it takes prohibited actions, but also that they will not
happen if it refrains. Thus we must pay more attention to convincing the Russians that, even in an extreme crisis, war is not
inevitable. Although to protect our basic values we must be
willing to risk war, we also need to show the Soviets that we are
willing to be reasonable and to respect their security. Living
with the chance of destruction will never be comfortable, but
Winston Churchill was right: safety can be the sturdy child of
terror.

ROBERT JERVIS

New York, New York

The Illogic of
American Nuclear Strategy

[1]

The Nuclear Revolution

A rational strategy for the employment of nuclear weapons is a contradiction in terms. The enormous destructive power of these weapons creates insoluble problems. For this reason, much of the history of nuclear strategy has been a series of attempts to find a way out of this predicament and return to the simpler, more comforting prenuclear world in which safety did not depend on the adversary's restraint. Short of developing an effective defense, however, these efforts cannot succeed. Instead, they can only produce doctrines which are incoherent and filled with contradictions, which though they are superficially alluring, upon close examination do not make sense. The problem is not that the people developing them have been thoughtless or lazy. Quite the opposite; the admirable aim to seek a way out of the conundrums that nuclear weapons present has been pursued with dedication, care, and logic. But the resulting policies inevitably will be deeply flawed unless they come to grips with the unfortunate fact that no strategy can provide the kind of protection that was possible in the past.

This, as I will seek to demonstrate in this book, is the fate of current American nuclear doctrine, the countervailing strategy. Contradictions are legion because security is pursued without full consideration of the ways in which nuclear weapons have altered world politics; the conclusions often ignore crucial factors because only by doing so can the analysis seem to solve the problems it has set for itself. To argue that any nuclear doctrine must be at least partly irrational does not mean that all doctrines are equally at odds with the reality they try to reflect and shape. If one starts with misleading conceptions, the more complete and thorough the reasoning, the stranger and more confused are the results. Only by understanding and accepting the implications of nuclear weapons can we develop a more appropriate policy. But even such a policy cannot meet all the standards we normally require of rationality. The situation we are in is not a rational one.

The countervailing strategy sees the need to meet potential Soviet threats on their own terms. The threat of all-out war, being suicidal, cannot deter lower levels of Soviet violence. The Russians will be deterred not—or at least not only—by the fear that aggression will lead to intolerable punishment (deterrence by punishment), but by the belief that the West can deny them any gains (deterrence by denial). American nuclear strategy has always sought deterrence through a combination of punishment and denial—the common belief that until the early 1960s the United States relied only on the threat of destroying Soviet cities is not correct.[1] But the stress has shifted to the importance of denial, as has been made clear by American war plans and statements under Nixon (the Schlesinger Doctrine), Carter (Presidential Directive [PD] 59), and Reagan. This makes sense in traditional military terms and this is why, as I will show, the policy is misguided. The alternative emphasizes punishment: the danger that aggression will lead to the destruction of the civilizations of both sides. Often known as the policy of Assured Destruction (AD) or Mutual Assured Destruction (MAD), this method of deterrence is now generally rejected because of its supposed lack of credibility. But I will argue that it is both inescapable and more potent than is often believed. The fact that cities are vulnerable and can be destroyed not only in mindless retaliation but also as the result of a series of actions not fully under the control of either side strongly inhibits either superpower from challenging the vital interests of the other.

IRRATIONALITY AND INTERNATIONAL POLITICS

Even before the era of weapons of mass destruction, action in the international arena was plagued by difficulties rarely encountered within states. The world lacks a central government; even if states want to cooperate, they may not be able to do so because they cannot be confident that others will cooperate with them. These difficulties are compounded by the security dilemma—that is, the tendency for policies that are aimed at increasing a state's security to have the effect (regardless of the intention) of decreasing the security of others.[2] Under these circumstances, the rational pursuit of self-interest by every state can make them all worse off than they would have been had they adopted alternative behavior. A variety of conditions affect the depth of this dilemma: for example, the balance between the efficacy of offensive and defensive military and political tactics, the specific pay-offs for the outcomes of the interactions, the ability of each state to determine what others are doing. But the essential point is that the international system may present states with enormous challenges to sensible policies.

This is indicated, for example, by the fact that states often pay more for objectives than they are worth. Of course similar situations occur in domestic politics—the phrase about throwing good money after bad was not coined by an international relations expert—but they are distressingly common in the international arena because of the lack of a sovereign who can regulate competition. Wars of attrition such as World War I fit this picture. As Thomas Schelling points out, "there is no logical reason why two adversaries will not bleed each other to death, drop by drop, each continually feeling that if he can only hold out a little longer, the other is bound to give in."[3]

[21]

THE NATURE OF THE NUCLEAR REVOLUTION

The development of nuclear weapons has operated to raise new barriers to a fully rational policy. Three factors are at work. The first, and most important, is the nuclear revolution: the enormous change in the way force can be used which follows from the inability of the superpowers to protect themselves from each other.[4] This is compounded by two others: the lack of empirical evidence on many crucial propositions and the increasing role of doctrine and beliefs in creating reality.

LACK OF PROPORTION BETWEEN MEANS AND ENDS

The nuclear revolution in turn can be separated into two related and familiar elements: the overwhelming power of the weapons and the existence of mutual second-strike capability, meaning that neither side can eliminate the other's retaliatory capacity by launching a disarming first strike. Not surprisingly, it was the power of the weapons that first caught attention. George Kennan pointed out the meaning of such power in a 1950 memorandum, which he later called the most important he ever wrote:

> . . . conventional weapons of warfare implied . . . that warfare should be a means to an end other than warfare, an end connected with the beliefs and the feelings and the attitudes of people, an end marked by submission to a new political will and perhaps to a new regime of life, but an end which at least did not negate the principle of life itself.
>
> The weapons of mass destruction do not have this quality. They reach backward beyond the frontiers of western civilization, to the concepts of warfare which were once familiar to the Asiatic hordes. They cannot really be reconciled with a political purpose directed to shaping, rather than destroying, the lives of the adversary. They fail to take account of the ultimate responsibility of men for one another, and even for each other's errors and mis-

takes. They imply the admission that man not only can be but is his own worst and most terrible enemy.[5]

The destructiveness of these weapons raises a number of linked issues. One is the ambiguity in our notions of the meaning of "power." Nuclear weapons obviously are extremely powerful in the sense of enabling those who possess them to destroy others and degrade the face of the planet. But it is much less clear that this ability can be translated into the power to affect others' behavior and reach many of the goals of statesmen. Perhaps we can kill but not influence, ruin civilizations but not alter policies, disrupt all patterns of human life but not change what others do in peacetime. Whether nuclear weapons are viewed as the most powerful force humans have ever invented or whether they are seen as quite ineffective, then, depends in part on what we mean when we raise the question of the nature of power.[6]

Although it is often true that the greater the power to harm others, the greater the power to affect their behavior, the relationship is not linear; past a certain point the ability to destroy may not be useful. The very extent of the destruction that would be wrought undermines the credibility of the threat to bring it about even if the other side cannot harm the attacking state in turn. Thus even if the United States had a nuclear monopoly, could it convince Nicaragua to cease supporting the rebels in El Salvador by threatening to wipe out Managua if it did not? Only part of the reason for a negative answer is that, even in the absence of retaliation, the United States might be harmed by the horrified reaction of third parties (even though others might be likely to comply with American wishes in the future). Probably more important is the pain that the American leaders and public would feel at killing large numbers of people—including innocent ones—in pursuit of a goal that was of less than supreme importance.

Of course this reason for restraint applies even without nuclear weapons. The United States could level Managua with

[23]

conventional bombs. The destructive power of nuclear bombs, however, is so great as to make such restraint of increased strength—which partly explains the puzzling lack of political advantage the atomic monopoly brought the United States. Although the stockpile was small in the Truman years and might not have been decisive in the event of war in any case,[7] the Russians may have shared the doubts held by Truman's advisers about whether he would allow the bomb to be used again. It was not until 1948 that the armed forces were permitted to plan for the possible use of atomic bombs, and even then Truman made clear that they could not count on his deciding to use them.[8] Only under Eisenhower, when the country was no longer the sole nuclear power, was it decided "that it is the policy of the United States to integrate atomic weapons with other weapons in the arsenal," and that "in the event of hostilities, the United States will consider nuclear weapons to be as available for use as other munitions."[9] And although Eisenhower may have threatened to use nuclear weapons against the Chinese if they refused to come to terms in Korea, even here, when retaliation was unlikely and emotions ran high because of prolonged fighting, it is far from clear that he would have carried out the threat.[10] These hesitations are not surprising; even when the other side cannot respond, as long as a state's leaders have some regard for humanity only the most vital of interests could call for unleashing unprecedented destruction.

The result is to render much of our prenuclear logic inadequate. As Bernard Brodie has stressed, the first question to ask about a war is what the political goal is that justifies the military cost.[11] When the cost is likely to be very high, only the most valuable goals are worth pursuing by military means. (It is partly on these grounds that many analysts doubt that the Soviet threat to vital American interests is particularly great. What prospective Soviet goals could possibly justify the risk of total destruction?) Of course, it can be argued that guaranteeing one's security by destroying one's major rival would be a goal worth killing many people. This may be true, but it is not certain that the use of nuclear weapons, even against a country without them, would reach that objective. If the United States had waged nuclear war against the Soviet Union before 1949, what would its war aims have been? What would it have done after destroying Soviet cities and armies? Could it have occupied, could it have controlled, the "smoking, radiating ruins"?[12] In fact, American officials saw these difficulties and set more modest wartime objectives.[13] But this line of argument would only raise more sharply the question of whether any achievable goals could justify the destruction.

Even though Truman claimed to have had no second thoughts about dropping atomic bombs on Japan, he understood the implications of the change in the scale of violence. As he told a close adviser: "It is a terrible thing to order the use of something that . . . is so terribly destructive, destructive beyond anything we have ever had. You have got to understand that this isn't a military weapon. It is used to wipe out women and children and unarmed people and not for military uses."[14] To put the point less graphically, the enormous amount of death and destruction which would be entailed by the use of nuclear weapons has brought an end to the proportionality between the means employed and the goals sought that used to characterize international politics.

Obviously, the largest issue raised by this lack of proportionality is whether nuclear weapons are compatible with the current system of nation-states. If warfare, which was once a normal instrument of statecraft, now threatens to destroy what it used to serve, should it not be altered or abandoned? One possibility, variants of which will be discussed throughout this book, is to limit the weapons by means of rules or of technology (building smaller and more accurate warheads) so that they can be made safe for use in warfare. Perhaps they can be made more usable by being made less destructive. If doing this is impossible, perhaps any use of them will become truly unthinkable. But if neither of these paths seems likely, may we not need to abolish or alter national sovereignty? After all, these

[25]

structures are not sacred; rather, they were designed to serve human life and well-being, and if they, like war, now threaten what they previously supported, should they not be adapted to the new situation? Thus Hans Morgenthau, who was best known for his emphasis on the role of power in international relations, came to see nuclear weapons as one of the crucial factors in rendering traditional views obsolete.

> Instead of trying in vain to assimilate nuclear power to the purposes and instrumentalities of the nation-state, we ought to have tried to adapt these purposes and instrumentalities to the potentialities of nuclear power. We have refrained from doing so in earnest, because to do so successfully requires a radical transformation—psychologically painful and politically risky—of traditional values, modes of thought and habits of action. But short of such a transformation, there will be no escape from the paradoxes of nuclear strategy and the dangers attending them.[15]

Similarly, George Kennan opened a recent article with a discussion of the need for world law, an idea that he and many others once thought "impractical, if not naive."[16]

MUTUAL KILL AND MUTUAL VULNERABILITY

The dilemmas are multiplied by the fact that both superpowers have large and secure nuclear forces. If the enormous levels of destructive power that nuclear bombs possess constitute one element of the nuclear revolution, the inability of either side to destroy all the other's strategic weapons forms the other element. The implications are well known: not overkill but mutual kill.[17] In the past, the side that won a major war could, if it chose, kill the losers. Now the losers can equally easily kill the winners. The forces that inflict damage on the adversary no longer protect the state, as they did in the past. Coercion, not brute force, deterrence, not defense, are the function of our weapons. Nuclear weapons cannot produce a victory the way superior military capability did in earlier eras. In the past, armies could operate by brute force—they could take and hold enemy territory, or, if they stood on the defensive, keep the enemy off their own land. They accomplished these ends by fighting and defeating the enemy's armies. This sort of encounter required no cooperation at all between the contending parties. None of this is true for strategic nuclear forces. They cannot directly take the other's territory or defend their own; the most appropriate targets are not—or at least are not only—the other's nuclear forces; even superior forces require that the other side cooperate if the military efforts are not to be in vain.

Nuclear force, then, operates through the ability to inflict pain and punishment on the other side. In earlier eras, this ability usually came only after the opponent's armies had been defeated. Now each superpower can hurt the other without destroying the latter's armed forces; at the same time, neither can prevent the other from hurting it by successfully attacking the other's weapons. This situation makes no sense in traditional military terms. On the one hand, the superpowers cannot directly protect their own populations; their military forces cannot accomplish what was their prime mission in the past. But they can destroy the other side, something that previously could be accomplished only after a state had defeated the other's armies and protected itself.

The result of mutual second-strike capability is that the superpowers must rely on deterrence rather than defense for their security. Of course, this is nothing entirely new; coercion was not born with nuclear weapons. The receiving and inflicting of punishment have always been inextricable parts of fighting. Combat depleted resources, killed soldiers, and severed beneficial economic relationships. On occasion, one or both sides believed that these costs would be so great that in the words of an eighteenth-century statesman, "it was little matter for whom victory declared, as ruin and destruction must be the inevitable consequences to both parties."[18] In other cases, one side felt that the costs would outrun the value of the prize, and so

[27]

accepted defeat or refused to embark on military adventures in which it could have succeeded. This was true, for example, of the United States in Vietnam. Military victory was possible, but was judged of insufficient value to outweigh the punishment inflicted by casualties, opposition from allies, and domestic unrest. The North Vietnamese were able to win not so much because their military capabilities were great, but because they were willing to bear unusual pain to reach their goal.[19] Similarly, the Japanese hoped to prevail in World War II not by physically preventing the United States from taking disputed territories, but by raising the price so high that the Americans would prefer to accept a limited defeat.

Furthermore, in earlier eras pain was not only a constant companion of combat, it was sometimes inflicted on purpose, as an easier or more effective way of gaining victory than defeating the other's armies. Laying waste farms and sacking cities to show the other side that the costs of continued fighting were greater than those of making concessions are time-honored tactics. The Prussians provided an example in 1871. As their armies swept through much of France they skirted fortified towns. But these had to be taken somehow, since they controlled key roads and were a threat to the Prussians' rear. To have besieged or stormed them would have been costly, and so instead they threatened to inflict pain by bombarding the cities with artillery.[20] And just as coercion was used in the past, so brute force is still used today. The ability of the Cuban soldiers to fight effectively obviously affected the outcomes of the conflicts in Angola and Ethiopia. The superpowers also can try to defeat an adversary's army. The United States did so in Grenada and could have won in Vietnam, even though the North had strong resolve and the U.S. was unwilling to suffer a high rate of casualties, if its strength had been sufficient to provide a quick and cheap victory.

But these continuities should not distract us from the main point. In most past cases, the option of defense was available, at least to one side. The stronger side could physically take what it sought and protect its own citizens and territory. The fact that this is no longer the case has caused a true revolution in strategy. The term "revolution" is often used quite loosely. Thus Henry Kissinger has called the Soviet development of MIRVs (multiple independently targeted reentry vehicles) "a strategic revolution," and Harold Brown refers to the development of the Dreadnought (the first battleship to carry only large and accurate guns) and torpedoes as "revolutionary changes."[21] But here I mean it seriously—as I will try to demonstrate throughout this book, mutual second-strike capability means that many things we used to take for granted are no longer true.

It is often said that the basic principles of nuclear strategy are quite simple: one merely takes common sense and turns it on its head. Of course this statement is exaggerated, but it is not a bad starting point. Recent American nuclear strategy, on the contrary, has tried to reassert the validity of prenuclear thinking. Although many of the details are arcane, its essentials are drawn from old truths. But rather than enhancing coherence in thinking and policy, the result has been to reduce it because the premises underlying this common sense are no longer valid. A better strategy must start with the realization that each side's civilization can be protected only by the other's cooperation. In such a world, the well-established idea that gaining a military advantage is necessary or sufficient for gaining security does not apply. As we shall see, many of the current strategic arguments stress the importance of the ability to destroy various Soviet military targets, or to destroy as many such targets as the Russians can destroy in turn. But the crucial links between these capabilities and deterring a war (or ending one on acceptable terms if it should occur) are rarely spelled out. When they are, they can be seen to rest on assumptions that mutual second-strike capability has invalidated.

Conflict and Cooperation:
The Stability-Instability Paradox

The nuclear revolution has had several other effects that make it difficult for a policy to meet normal standards of ra-

[29]

tionality. To start with, both conflict and cooperation between the superpowers have been raised to unprecedented heights. Some commentators stress that nuclear weapons increase the conflict between nations, pointing to the tensions, threats, and competition that characterize the Cold War as well as to the elemental fact that each side can destroy the other. Furthermore, the importance of judgments about the other's resolve means that small issues are seen as having major consequences. Statesmen often feel that in order to protect their vital interests they must demonstrate their willingness to risk war, which in turn requires belligerent tactics and a refusal to make more than minimal concessions. To be reasonable in one case may undermine one's position in later confrontations. Other analysts have drawn different implications from the possibility of mutual destruction, arguing that the level of cooperation is now much higher than in the past because the superpowers can survive only by working together.

In fact, the impulses toward cooperation and toward conflict have both been strengthened. Far from creating a zero-sum situation, as many criticisms of deterrence policies imply, nuclear weapons create an unprecedented common interest between the two adversaries. Their fates are linked together—or the fate of each is in the other's hands—in a way that was never true in the past. Indeed, if the environmental effects of a nuclear war, such as the depletion of the ozone layer of the upper atmosphere or the creation of soot which would block most sunlight, would be so severe that any widespread use of nuclear weapons would destroy all nations, then even a militarily successfully disarming strike would be suicidal.[22] This interdependence, however, does not reliably lead to cooperation. The shared common interest of avoiding all-out war can be competitively exploited because achieving this goal requires that only one side, not both, makes concessions. Indeed, the very strength of the shared incentives not to let a conflict lead to war permits the side with greater resolve—or foolhardiness—to shift to the adversary the burden of avoiding mutual destruction. Conflict and cooperation, always intertwined in the past, are now knotted together even more tightly. As a result, states are under especially great, and especially contradictory, pressures. War must be avoided, but to follow this imperative too openly is to invite exploitation. The other side's need to avoid war can be used for leverage, but pushing too hard can lead to the worst outcome of all.

One result of the tight links between incentives to cooperate and incentives to exploit the other is what Glenn Snyder has called the stability-instability paradox.[23] To the extent that the military balance is stable at the level of all-out nuclear war, it will become less stable at lower levels of violence. That is, if an uncontrolled war would lead to mutual destruction, then neither side should ever start one. But this very stability allows either side to use limited violence because the other's threat to respond by all-out retaliation cannot be very credible. If the strategic balance were unstable and both sides feared that an increase in tensions could lead to World War III, then fierce competition would be seen as more dangerous, and more moderate behavior would be induced. But to the extent that all-out war is unthinkable, states have greater opportunities to push as hard as they can. The problem is brought out nicely by Bernard Brodie, who argues for the existence of "a common recognition, among those powers possessing substantial nuclear capabilities, that thermonuclear war between them is simply forbidden, and thus also lesser wars that might too easily lead up to the large-scale thermonuclear variety."[24] But if an all-out war is simply "forbidden," does this not make "lesser wars" relatively safe? Of course "relatively safe" may not be safe enough and even a slightly credible threat of all-out war may be credible enough to deter the other side. But the paradox cannot be completely disposed of in this manner; there remains a trade-off between the perceived risk of total conflict and the possibilities for adventurism.

The anomalous nature of this situation is also revealed in Brodie's analysis of the Cuban missile crisis. This confrontation, he argues, "shows a remarkably different quality from any previous one in history. There is an unprecedented candor, direct personal contact, and at the same time mutual respect between the chief actors. . . . Both sides at once agree that their quarrel could lead to nuclear war, which is impossible to contemplate and which would leave no winner. In effect they were asking each other: How do we get out of this with the absolute minimum of damage to each other including each other's prestige?" But even though the United States made some concessions, the final outcome was more an American victory than a compromise, as Brodie himself notes two pages later. The fact that both sides wanted to avoid war meant that the one more willing to risk this outcome could shift onto the other's shoulders the costs of retreating.[25]

The stability-instability paradox is a product of being in a Chicken situation—that is, one in which extreme conflict is both sides' last choice—and so anything that might lead to such a situation will have the same dynamics even if nuclear weapons are not involved. An interesting example is the question whether the Soviets were implicated in the attempt on the pope's life. Most people find the idea implausible because the Russians would pay such a high price were others to discover their role. But if other states acknowledge their belief that the Russians were involved, they would have to damage their relations with the Soviet Union. If they do not want to do this, then the others would hesitate to admit they think the Russians were involved. If the Russians anticipated this reaction, they might have believed the costs of assassinating the pope to be relatively low and so might have carried out the adventure.

The most familiar form of this problem is the difficulty of providing extended deterrence, that is, deterring attacks on allies. If all-out war means the destruction of the United States, would not American leaders prefer to see Western Europe conquered by the Russians—bad as that outcome would be—rather than attacking the USSR with nuclear weapons and having the Russians retaliate? Taking this logic a step further, some have argued that mutual second-strike capability makes incredible the American threat to destroy Russian cities in response to a Soviet attack limited to U.S. strategic forces. Much of the intellectual power of current American strategic doctrine derives from an appreciation of the stability-instability paradox. I will argue later that these views overlook crucial considerations of risk and chance, but the problem is still a basic characteristic of the nuclear era.

The same incentives operate in Soviet-American competition in the Third World, albeit with less intensity. According to Coit Blacker, some Soviet analysts argue that "prior to the arrival of strategic parity . . . , the Kremlin had been deterred in many instances from challenging U.S. policy or from assisting those elements opposed to imperialism."[26] With the American nuclear threat neutralized by the Soviet counterthreat, the Russians are freed from one of the inhibitions against intervention in underdeveloped countries, especially if direct clashes with U.S. forces are avoided.

The contrasting pressures produced by the magnification of both conflict and cooperation also create contradictory incentives for specific tactics. When the costs of going to war are so high, the threat do so is undermined. Credibility then becomes both crucial and problematical. States use—and are forced to use—tactics designed to convince the other that mutual disaster will result if the latter does not make concessions.[27] Thus in a crisis states often commit themselves to standing firm. This increases the chance that the other will retreat, but also—and for this reason the tactic produces leverage—increases the costs the state will pay if it is the one forced to back down. The other side is also likely to retreat if a statesman convinces it that he is foolish or blind to the dangers. Thus H. R. Haldeman reported that President Nixon sought to lead the North Vietnamese to believe that he was unpredictable and could not be counted on to be sensibly restrained.[28] But this "rationality of irrationality," as Schelling terms it, may lead the other side not to retreat, but to strike in the belief that war is inevitable. Credibility can perhaps also be bolstered by showing how much pain a state is willing to bear on minor issues. Others may then reason that it will run even higher risks and pay higher costs in more significant confrontations. This is one reason why states are often willing to pay a price greater than the value of fairly small stakes. But all these tactics introduce further elements of irrationality. They call for reducing cooperation and predictability and increasing the costs to both sides. Furthermore, a record of using them may make it harder to reach compromises during crises and to develop mutually beneficial understanding during normal times.

In the event of war between the superpowers, similar conflicting incentives would operate. Violence would have to be carefully limited and controlled to avoid suicide; yet it is the possibility of that outcome which would produce so much pressure for a settlement. To eschew the most powerful weapons in one's arsenal would be to limit one's military potential; to use the weapons would invite a reply in kind. To take the sharpest example, to attack the other side's command, control, communication, and intelligence facilities (C^3I) might be the only chance for victory, but it would also increase the chance that the adversary will launch an unrestrained counterattack.

The Search for Implementable Options

The most important consequence of the nuclear revolution follows from the linked but opposed facts that each side can protect its cities only with the cooperation of its adversary but that each can defend its interests only at some risk of catastrophic war. The ultimate threat that deters each from infringing on the other's vital interests is the fear the result of the conflict will be the destruction of both societies. In the absence of effective defenses, no military options and military abilities can prevent this outcome. The other side will always be able to attack the initiating state's civilization; only bargaining, not force, can dissuade it from doing so. This means that for the state to confront the other is to face the danger of all-out war. Because escalation, which would ruin both sides, is an ever-present possibility, attempts to put pressure on the other side during a crisis will also put pressure on the state itself.

This is the foundation of the inescapable dilemmas we face. The main point can be seen in the problem with Secretary of Defense Brown's claim that "credibility cannot be maintained, especially in a crisis, with a combination of inflexible forces (however destructive) and a purely counter-urban industrial strategic option that *frightens us as much as the opponent.*"29 As long as American cities are in hostage, it is hard to see what strategy would not frighten us as much as it would the Russians. For what is most frightening is not the immediate result of the use of force against the Soviet Union, but rather the chance that the final result would be our own destruction. One side may be more willing to run this risk than the other, and this will be an important influence on the course of a crisis, but since each can destroy the other and cannot protect itself, major threats must involve the possibility that both sides will suffer extreme losses.30

The same problem is raised by the claim that, in the words of Secretary of Defense James Schlesinger, "we require a nuclear capability that has an implementable threat and which is perceived to have an implementable threat. Unless, in the event of certain hostile acts, we have a threat that we can implement, the existence of the American force structure does not contribute logically to deterrence."31 Without threats that are more than mere bluffs, he argued, American influence cannot be brought to bear. As Henry Kissinger put it in a formulation endorsed by the Carter administration: "The side that can defend its interests only by threatening to initiate the mutual mass extermination of civilians will gradually slide toward strategic and, therefore, geopolitical paralysis."32 Caspar Weinberger has similarly argued that "if our threatened response is perceived as . . . contrary to our national interest, it will be judged to be a bluff."33 But the ability to carry out threats of limited destruction does not deal with the basic fact that one's cities are still in hostage. The chance that civilization will be destroyed if the crisis escalates exerts great pressures on both sides to reduce the risk of war; having multiple options greatly decreases these pressures only if a state is confident that its adversary will be restrained. In the past, states that were stronger than their adversaries could credibly threaten major war because if the other did not comply, the threat could rationally be carried out. Threats were then "implementable" in the sense Schlesinger presumably intended.[34] Since states can no longer protect themselves, this is no longer the case.

The same kind of conceptual confusion is revealed when Weinberger argues that "we must . . . make sure that the Soviet leadership, in calculating the risks of aggression, recognizes that an effective American response exists."[35] This requirement seems straightforward, indeed almost self-evident. But what would an "effective response" be? Presumably one that stopped the Russians from undertaking or continuing undesired behavior. But the nuclear revolution means that neither side has a response that can prevent the other from destroying its civilization. Furthermore, the possibility of total war means that responses to lower levels of aggression that might seem "effective" in the narrow sense of preventing the other from making gains are very dangerous because the conflict could escalate. Thus the fact that "an American response exists" in these cases may not provide deterrence because the threat to respond may not be credible. These problems are disguised by the terms and approaches used in recent U.S. defense policy. The traditional way in which threats were "implementable" and "geopolitical paralysis" was avoided—being strong enough so that it was in one's interest to engage in major war if need be—is simply no longer available.

The difficulties involved are clearly brought out by Henry Kissinger's reported reaction to the military's attempt to provide limited nuclear options that could be employed in the event of a Soviet invasion of Iran. The first plan called for the United States to drop nearly two hundred bombs on Russian military targets adjacent to the Iranian border. According to Fred Kaplan, Kissinger was horrified: "Are you out of your minds? This is a *limited* option?" But he was no more impressed when the military planners returned with the idea of a much smaller strike limited to the two main roads leading from Russia to Iran.

> The new proposal called for exploding an atomic demolition mine on one of the roads and firing two nuclear weapons at the other. Again, Kissinger's eyes impatiently rolled toward the ceiling. "What kind of nuclear attack is this?" he demanded. The U.S. takes the terrible risk of going nuclear and then uses only two weapons? Kissinger [said] . . . that if the United States carried out such a plan and if he were Brezhnev, he would conclude that the American President was "chicken."[36]

Both reactions may have been correct. One cannot possibly make sense out of the use of nuclear weapons in traditional military terms; no one can say with any confidence "how much use would be enough." The utility of limited nuclear options (and, indeed, even of conventional violence) depends less on military effect than on resolve and images of resolve.

In this situation, we must ask a series of questions for any proposed nuclear strategy: If the United States cannot take its cities out of hostage, what does it want to threaten and do to the Russians? If the threat to destroy Soviet society is believed to be inadequate, what missions do American forces need to be able to carry out? Why would the threat to attack various targets be credible and efficacious? How would the threat or its implementation contribute to successful termination of a war? As I will demonstrate, approaching these questions without understanding that mutual vulnerability has altered the way force can be used will lead to incoherent answers and self-defeating policies.

PAUCITY OF EVIDENCE AND THE ENLARGED ROLE OF BELIEFS

The primary cause of our predicament is the nuclear revolution, but, as I mentioned, two other factors compound it: the

[37]

lack of empirical evidence on many crucial points, and the role of beliefs and doctrine in creating rather than mirroring reality. Effective conventional military doctrines are at least in part the product of hundreds of years of experience. Although our knowledge is far from complete, at least we can examine large numbers of instances of war, escalation, threats, bluffs, and terminations of wars. Our knowledge of nuclear deterrence, by contrast, is largely deductive. We have a number of plausible theories, but only very limited empirical evidence.[37]

The paucity of evidence about the effect of alternative nuclear strategies feeds the enlarged role of doctrines and beliefs. To a greater extent than was true in the past, they now shape, rather than describe, reality. Of course people's beliefs are always at least a proximate cause of their behavior. Thus the mobilization races in July 1914 and some of what we would now call the "crisis instablity" of that period can only be explained by the participants' beliefs—which turned out to be incorrect—that the side which struck first would gain a great advantage.[38] But we can at least talk about the objective reality that these beliefs reflected and filtered. For many vital questions of strategy, we can no longer do so. On such matters as whether nuclear war can be kept limited, whether a threat is credible, and how many weapons are enough to enable a state to stand firm, there is no reality to be described that is independent of people's beliefs about it.

One cannot even say that these questions have objective answers that could be determined by the course of an actual war, because the way such a war would be fought and its outcome would depend in part on beliefs. To take one example, the belief that armed conflict can be kept limited is a necessary, although not a sufficient, condition, for keeping it controlled. Furthermore, to think that it can be controlled also implies that the other shares this view and knows that the first side realizes it does (or will develop these beliefs during the prewar crisis).

Similarly, the question of what kinds of threats are credible cannot be completely answered without considering the participants' beliefs. There are not likely to be deterministic links between statesmen's views about how the other side will react and objective and "underlying" variables like the distribution of military power and the relative value that each side places in the issue at stake. Much depends on autonomous ideas. For example, a decision-maker who thinks that messages communicated publicly are more serious than those conveyed in secret will believe certain threats which others who had the opposite belief would disregard. Statesmen who think that the world is tightly interconnected through the medium of states' reputations for living up to their words will make commitments in the expectation that others are not likely to challenge them and, conversely, will expect others to fulfill promises and threats when they have staked their signaling reputations on doing so. Decision-makers who believe that these reputations are relatively unimportant will neither rely on the tactic of commitment nor believe that others are especially likely to follow a course of action just because they have pledged themselves to do so. Of course, in the past, beliefs on these matters were not uniform and completely determined by objective factors. But the whole notion of credibility was more straightforward when it could be in a state's interest to implement the warnings it issues. To the extent this is no longer the case, credibility becomes at once more important and more elusive, thereby giving greater insight to beliefs about what makes threats believable.

Beliefs also influence the crucial question of the impact of the nuclear balance on political outcomes. If one side thinks it has a usable military advantage, it is more likely to stand firm in a confrontation. (It may also be more likely to follow an adventurist foreign policy, although the contrary reaction is possible as well: it may believe that it is strong and secure enough to be moderate. Here a lot depends on the state's intentions.) If the state also believes that the other side shares this perception of advantage, it will think that the adversary is more likely to retreat, and so it will be even more likely to stand firm. The other side of this coin is that states which think they are weak will be "self-deterred."[39]

That beliefs have this sort of importance raises an interesting

[39]

question that cannot be fully explored here. How much influence have deterrence theorists had over the behavior they are seeking to explain? Have U.S. beliefs and policies created a self-fulfilling prophecy? Certain postures could be necessary for the self-confidence of decision-makers because they have accepted notions propounded by academics. To the extent that theorists can influence beliefs and doctrines, they affect what they are analyzing. They do so, furthermore, whether they seek the role or not.

Related here is the tension between the argument that the nuclear revolution is an objective fact and the claim that doctrines and beliefs play a large role in shaping not only perceptions of reality, but reality itself. If everyone denied the importance of the change introduced by nuclear weapons, if no one grasped the significance of mutual vulnerability, then indeed there would be more continuity between the current situation and prenuclear ones. But even a minimal understanding of these matters limits the scope for doctrinal influence. This is especially true because in moments of confrontation and crisis the significance of mutual vulnerability bears in on decision-makers. I noted that if statesmen believed that whichever side was "ahead" according to various indicators of military power would prevail during a crisis or limited war, then these indicators would matter just as it would matter if they believed that whichever side wore better clothing had the advantage. But the former advantage can no more unilaterally protect one's civilization than the latter, and this point is universally accepted even though its implications may not be. Thus while a denial of the importance of the revolution can influence behavior, it cannot shape the world entirely to the choosing of those who hold these views. As Brodie put it when rejecting the claim that limited nuclear options could bring flexibility to the strategic arena: "The rigidity lies in the situation, not in the thinking."[40]

To argue the centrality of the nuclear revolution is to deny the common claim that the root causes of current dilemmas lie in any one of four factors: changing technology, Soviet military doctrine, Soviet nuclear "superiority," and American alliance commitments. This is not to say that these factors have not magnified the obstacles to a coherent and effective policy, but to argue that they have often received too much blame. Were they to be more propitious, the world would be only slightly safer.

It is widely believed that the rapid pace of technological progress since 1945 requires equally rapid change in basic ideas. For example, in the bibliography of *Nuclear Weapons and Foreign Policy*, Henry Kissinger refers to Brodie et al., *The Absolute Weapon* as "dated."[41] Since these essays were an early and terribly prescient analysis of the effects of nuclear weapons, Kissinger's evaluation of them is symptomatic. Indeed most of his writings fail to grasp the essentials of the nuclear revolution. The technological changes which had occurred between the time of Brodie's essays and Kissinger's book a decade later were significant. But they did not alter the crucial points. The most important developments were the invention of the hydrogen bomb, the growth of the nuclear stockpile, and the progress of the Soviet program; but they only brought the revolution to full fruition.

In recent years, much attention has been focused on the destabilizing influence of rapidly changing technology, particularly on the development of highly accurate MIRVs. If only we had been able to freeze technology in the 1960s, it is argued, our plight would be greatly eased because neither side could hope to destroy more of the other's warheads than it would use in its own strike. If only states did not have to worry about the new tricks that unfolding technology might play—and the opportunities it may provide—much of the pressure for new programs and new doctrines would abate. There is something to this, but it obscures the crucial point that when both sides have second-strike capability, threats to use extreme violence are questionable. The search for flexibility, for "implementable options," for things that would be sensible to do if deterrence failed, is the product of the stability of the overall nuclear balance, not the slight instabilities in portions of it. The theoretical vulnerability of the American—and Soviet—land-based forces is troublesome, but this problem is quite independent of most of those considered in the rationales for the current countervailing strategy, which will be discussed below. Those problems would remain even if we had the 1960s technology, which now looks so attractive to arms controllers.

The obverse is that new technologies (excepting an effective defense) will not remove most of our difficulties because they will not take cities out of hostage or greatly reduce the dangers of engaging in violence that could escalate. Thus while the deployment of a new generation of missiles which were both invulnerable and, because of having only one warhead, unable to destroy a disproportionate number of the other side's missiles would be welcomed because it would eliminate[42] the incentives for either side to strike first in a crisis, it would leave untouched the basic dilemmas of how to use the threat of nuclear war to ensure security when such a war would be suicidal. Similarly, even if technology were to move in a different direction and the United States were to develop warheads so accurate that they could carry conventional explosives to selected targets such as silos or KGB headquarters, deterrence would not necessarily grow easier since these weapons would not protect American cities.

Soviet military doctrine, which seems to deny the distinction between deterrence and defense and which rejects the claim that mutual assured destruction (MAD) supplies a firm foundation for mutual security, also poses problems for American security, but even if both sides espoused MAD, the opportunities for exploitation of the common interest of avoiding mutual destruction would remain. The fact that American cities are vul-

[42]

nerable, not the way the Russians might employ force, is the main source of the difficulties I have noted.

Again, I am not denying that this factor can be a complicating one. The Soviet offensive doctrine in Europe is alarming, especially because it does not seem the best suited to serve legitimate Russian security needs. Problems are created by what seems to be the Soviet view that one side can become more secure only by making the other less so. To the extent that the Russians believe that security grows out of the ability to do better than the adversary in a war—and it is not certain that this is an accurate characterization of the Soviet view—then an element of competitiveness will always be present in Soviet-American military relations even if Soviet and American political goals are compatible. In other words, even if the Russians are not aggressive, their believing that their security requires superiority would be quite troublesome. But it would not necessarily make them harder to deter or force the United States to renounce any of its commitments. Although the Soviet equation of deterrence with defense may drive the USSR to higher levels of military spending and contribute to its own feelings of insecurity, it is not responsible for most of the dilemmas confronting Western defense policies. A Soviet doctrine that could assuage the fears which drive the countervailing strategy is hard to imagine, since the stability-instability paradox is not a function of the Soviet approach to deterrence.

Putative Soviet nuclear superiority is also commonly cited as a cause of many American problems. Many analysts would agree with Henry Kissinger that "it is urgently necessary either that the Soviets be deprived of their counter-force capability . . . or that a U.S. counter-force capability . . . be rapidly built."[43] The Carter administration seemed to concur in principle if not in detail: its development of the countervailing strategy coincided with the growing acceptance of the view that the Soviets were deploying more, and more effective, nuclear forces than the United States. Furthermore, much recent rhetoric suggests that

[43]

many American programs, such as the MX, are necessary only because the Soviets have similar systems. But the major challenges to U.S. policy come not from Soviet superiority, but from parity: that is, the development of Soviet second-strike capability. Indeed the idea of limited options began in the late 1950s and early 1960s when analysts looked ahead, not to Soviet superiority, but to the era of parity. It was widely believed that this condition would undercut the American threat of massive retaliation against attacks on its allies. Superiority without the ability to protect one's civilization does not give either side much leverage. Drawing even with the Soviets—assuming that they are indeed ahead of us—would not alter the vulnerability of American cities, and it is this which inhibits the United States from using force under circumstances which could lead to all-out war.

If one believes that the United States needs the ability to launch a first nuclear strike to compensate for weaknesses in local defenses, then matching the Soviets on various indicators of nuclear power is insufficient and the solution must be usable American superiority. This is implicit in Kissinger's argument about the military posture needed to sustain American foreign policy: "it was in [the Western] interest to maintain for as long as possible a counterforce capability [against Russian ICBMs]. . . . So long as the Soviets had to fear a counterforce attack in response to local aggression, their inhibition against such adventures would be considerable."[44] This position has a high degree of logical integrity, but it is contrary both to the common diagnosis of the problems facing the United States and to the arms-control principles that the United States espouses.

The need to deter attacks against allies similarly cannot account for the supposed need for multiple options and the ability to match the Soviets at any level of violence, although this need does establish additional hurdles for U.S. policy.[45] First, it should be noted that the problem of extended deterrence does not exist for interests that are seen as truly vital. That is, if Persian Gulf oil is seen as necessary for American independence or if Europe is seen as a part of the United States, deterring attacks on these areas is no more difficult than deterring attacks on the homeland; the question "would the president sacrifice New York for Paris or Bonn?" would not raise issues different from "would the president sacrifice New York for Detroit, the ICBM field in Montana, or any other American target which had been destroyed?" Of course in the latter case nuclear weapons would already have been used against some parts of the United States, but would this be more of a provocation or more of a loss than if Europe were being overrun? An attack on Europe would appear to the Russians less risky than a direct attack on U.S. territory only if they believed that Washington was willing to live with a Soviet-controlled Europe but not with the results of a Soviet strike against the United States. One can also argue that even if the Russians see Europe as vital to the United States, deterrence is difficult because Europe, unlike the American homeland, is vulnerable to an attack by conventional forces. But it is the outcome more than the weapons employed which is repugnant to the United States. Furthermore, although a Soviet conventional attack on Europe would require the United States to take the nuclear initiative whereas a direct Soviet strike against the United States would shift the onus of crossing the nuclear threshold to the Russians, the former action also requires the Soviets to make an incredibly risky move.

The protection of very important, but less than vital, interests is difficult, although not as difficult as is often believed. American analysts tend to focus on the constraints on an American strategic nuclear response to a Soviet conventional invasion of Europe. Many would presumably rate the chance of such a response as fairly low, say, 1 chance out of 4. But this number would look very different from the Soviet perspective. It is hard to argue that for the Soviet Union Europe is worth a 25 percent chance of the destruction of its society. Furthermore, while the American threat to use nuclear weapons if Europe were attacked is presumably less credible than the threat to do so in response to an attack on its own homeland, less credibility is necessary. That is, since conquering Europe would be worth less to Russia than destroying the United States, deterrence does not require as powerful a threat in the former case as it does in the latter.

It is also important to realize that even if American overseas commitments disappeared and the country were a self-sufficient island, the logic of current American doctrine implies that the United States would need to be able to meet the danger of Soviet nuclear blackmail aimed at altering its policies and behavior. The vulnerability of U.S. cities could be used to extract concessions. Although resisting such compellent threats is made easier by the fact that the status quo would remain unless the state being threatened believed that its adversary would dare to take a very dangerous move to alter it, the stability-instability paradox still operates and, if the premises of the countervailing strategy are accepted, requires strenuous efforts to control.[46] Herman Kahn's distinction between Type I deterrence (which deters a direct attack on one's homeland) and Type II deterrence (which deters "extreme provocations" such as an attack on Europe), while useful for preliminary discussion, is too crude for more careful and complete analysis.[47]

In summary, while these four factors create difficulties, even without them the basic dilemmas created by the nuclear revolution would remain. Since it is the attempt to escape from these dilemmas that motivates current policy, most of the rationales for it would make as much sense as they do now if technology, Soviet doctrine and forces, and American commitments all posed fewer problems than they now do.

[2]

Tensions and Attempted Escapes

The changes brought about by nuclear weapons are so painful and difficult that it is not surprising that people react not by
making the best of the new realities, but by seeking alluring, if
ultimately misleading, paths which they think will lead back to
traditional security. In the last chapter we saw one aspect of
this, the incorrect identification of the source of many of our
defense problems. Here I want to present other signs of the
dilemmas that nuclear weapons create and discuss the reactions
produced. The situation of mutual vulnerability is frightening
and unfamiliar and therefore has led to tensions and inconsistencies in people's beliefs and numerous attempts to deny or
escape from the situation. Because nuclear weapons both promise safety through deterrence and involve the chance of total
destruction, our beliefs about them contain severe tensions.
Because the deficiencies of any policy, even—or perhaps especially—ones we believe in, are apparent, most analysts have
changed their minds on some of the most important issues.
What is most striking: because dealing with the nuclear revolution is so difficult, people have tried to escape from it in a
variety of ways, none of which can work but some of which
form the basis for current policy.

THE BUILT-IN TENSIONS OF THE NUCLEAR REVOLUTION

One manifestation of the difficulty of constructing a sensible
nuclear policy is a series of tensions and trade-offs that cannot

[47]

be completely resolved. These are created by the conflicts between the destructive power of the weapons, which makes them unusable, and the need to make them serve political goals. Nuclear weapons are simultaneously crucial to and set apart from normal politics. The starting point was put well by Brodie: "It is the curious paradox of our time that one of the foremost factors making deterrence really work and work well is the lurking fear that in some massive confrontation crisis it might fail. Under these circumstances one does not tempt fate."[1] But as I noted, stability at the strategic nuclear level can lead to instability at lower levels of violence. Thus a tension is created between the desire to make the strategic balance as stable as possible in order to decrease the chance of all-out war and the desire to use strategic forces to deter less than total assaults. The more we reduce the incentives to strike first and decrease the risks that things will get out of control in a crisis, the less useful our strategic forces become in all but the most extreme and unlikely contingencies.[2] But to increase the usable scope of our deterrent in a world of mutual vulnerability means increasing the chance that, if the threat is not believed, the result will be world war.

A second and related tension is that statesmen are torn between supporting deterrence by underlining the threat that what the other side values will be destroyed if major war breaks out and the desire to minimize damage if conflict actually erupts.[3] In the past, on occasions when military victory was possible, states threatened to do what would be in their interests if the other was recalcitrant: go to war and fight simultaneously to protect themselves and to weaken the other side. Now, however, when the possibilities of punishment are mutual and divorced from progress on the battlefield, there is a contradiction between what each side wants to convince the other is likely to happen in the event of war and what each would like to have happen if fighting starts.

The reaction of the European members of NATO to various American defense plans brings out this tension particularly sharply. The European governments oppose almost every

[48]

change the United States puts forward, regardless of its content, and usually support the status quo, whatever that is. They don't want the United States to send more nuclear weapons to Europe; they don't want them to take many out. They don't want more efforts devoted to conventional defense; they don't want fewer troops. Although much of their position can be explained by their domestic politics and the relative freedom enjoyed by smaller powers, in part it reflects the tension between the threat they want to make and what they would want to happen in the event of aggression. On the one hand, to minimize the risk that war would be fought on their territory, the Europeans want to make the Russians believe that such a conflict would lead to devastation of the Soviet homeland. On the other hand, they do not want to see NATO rely totally on nuclear weapons because this would ensure that if war came, damage would be total. European decision-makers have tended to differ from American in opting for greater stress on the threat of all-out war both because they seem to take the Soviet threat and American diplomatic skill less seriously than do the Americans and because for them the trade-off is not the same, since they would bear the costs of a war limited to the Continent. But statesmen on both sides of the Atlantic—and in the Soviet Union—feel conflicting pressures.

The third tension is implicit in the previous discussion— states may be able to increase the chance of peace only by increasing the chance that war, if it comes, will be total. To decrease the probability of enormous destruction may increase the probability of aggression and limited wars. This can be called "the great trade-off" because the values involved are so crucial. A policy that simultaneously minimized the dangers of aggression, limited war, and all-out war would of course be desirable, but mutual vulnerability has put this happy configuration out of reach. We may be able to purchase gains of one major value only by sacrifices of another, a situation of psychological strain that is often met by refusal to recognize the painful choice.[4]

A fourth tension springs from the previous three: decision-

[49]

makers have been torn between, on the one hand, treating nuclear bombs as weapons not qualitatively different from others that are usable in a range of conflicts and, on the other hand, seeing them as unique, essentially untamable, and cut off from normal politics. To adopt the former position calls for the development of technologies, rules, and understandings that could permit the weapons to be used without destroying what they are supposed to protect.[5] It also increases the danger that the weapons *will* be used because the parties may believe that the costs and risks are not out of proportion to the values at stake. But to see nuclear weapons as in a category by themselves raises the problem that these arms would deter only a full-scale attack on the homeland and could not protect allies and combat blackmail. This issue was eloquently addressed by George Kennan in the 1950 memorandum already mentioned, which merits quoting at length:

> The problem is: for what purpose, and against the background of what subjective attitude, are we to develop such weapons and to train our forces in their use?
>
> We may regard them as something vital to our conduct of a future war—as something without which our war plans would be emasculated and ineffective—as something which we have resolved, in the face of all the moral and other factors concerned, to employ forthwith and unhesitatingly at the outset of any great military conflict. In this case, we should take the consequences of that decision now, and we should obviously keep away from any program of international dealings which would bring us closer to the possibility of agreement on international control and prohibition of the atomic weapon.
>
> Or we may regard them as something superfluous to our basic military posture—as something which we are compelled to hold against the possibility that they might be used by our opponents. In this case, of course, we take care not to build up a reliance upon them in our military planning. Since they then represent only a burdensome expenditure of funds and effort, we hold only the minimum required for the deterrent-retaliatory purpose. And we are at liberty, if we so desire, to make it our objective to divest ourselves of this minimum at the earliest moment by achieving a scheme of international control. . . .

. . . If we decide to hold weapons of mass destruction only for deterrent-retaliatory purposes, then the limit on the number and power of the weapons we should hold is governed by our estimate as to what it would take to make attack on this country or its allies by weapons of mass destruction a risky, probably unprofitable, and therefore irrational undertaking for any adversary. In these circumstances, the problem of whether to develop the superbomb and other weapons of mass destruction becomes only a question of the extent to which they would be needed to achieve this purpose. . . .

If, on the other hand, we are resolved to use weapons of mass destruction deliberately and prior to their use against us or our allies, in a future war, then our purpose is presumably to inflict maximum destruction on the forces, population and territory of the enemy, with the least expenditure of effort, in full acceptance of the attendant risk of retaliation against us, and in the face of all moral and political considerations. In this case, the only limitations on the number and power of mass destruction weapons which we would wish to develop would presumably be those of ordinary military economy, such as cost, efficiency, and ease of delivery.[6]

The irreconcilable tension is neatly caught by two of Truman's remarks in early 1949. David Lilienthal records that in one conversation Truman "began by saying that the atomic bomb was the mainstay and all he had; that the Russians would probably have taken over Europe a long time ago if it were not for that." Five days later, when talking with Lilienthal about how many bombs could be produced by the beginning of 1951, he said: "wouldn't it be wonderful when January 1, 1951, comes around, if we could take the whole business and dump it into the sea?"[7] This tension has never been resolved because it cannot be. The weapons hold out the possibility for such destruction as to make them radically different from conventional ones. But even if the United States tried to restrict its reliance on them, the fact that they could be used gives them influence over a range of contingencies and creates obvious pressures to render them usable.

Another sign of the difficulties of our situation is that analysts are inconsistent, changing their minds in ways that cannot easily be accounted for by new ideas, technologies, or events. The explanation lies, I think, in the tensions just discussed, coupled with the lack of empirical evidence. For example, in his first book on nuclear weapons, Henry Kissinger kept shifting his assumptions about the propensity of Soviet leaders to take risks. Thus he argued that undertaking mobilization might trigger a Russian attack, but that it would be possible to fight limited nuclear wars.[8] Both arguments have some plausibility, but they do not fit together well. If the situation is so unstable that mobilization could lead to preemption, it could not support a controlled nuclear war. President Eisenhower displayed a similar inconsistency. In 1956 he told his advisers that "the tactical use of atomic weapons against military targets would be no more likely to trigger off a big war than the use of twenty-ton 'block busters.'" But later, in reference to the Berlin crisis, he said: "If resort to arms should become necessary, our troops in Berlin would be quickly overrun, and the conflict would almost inevitably be global war."[9] Bernard Brodie shifted the stress he put on the elements of conflict and cooperation in extreme crisis. Six months after the Cuban missile crisis he wrote that Kennedy "face[d] up last October to a maneuver that entailed in his mind some risk of general war" and thereby gained a diplomatic victory. But ten years later he wrote that both sides were so concerned with the danger of nuclear war during the crisis that they worked together to find a way out, taking care to respect each other's interests.[10] Thus even starting from the same point—the importance of the risk of general war—Brodie reached inconsistent conclusions.

Analysts have also changed positions on more concrete issues. For years, most high officials insisted that Minuteman vulnerability was a grave problem. They argued that because of accurate MIRVs, the Russians could use a relatively small proportion of their missiles to destroy almost all the American intercontinental ballistic missiles (ICBMs), and they rejected the rebuttal that such an attack, even if successful, would involve risks out of all proportion to the gains because many of the bombers and submarine-launched ballistic missiles (SLBMs) would survive. But in accepting the Scowcroft report, which was issued in April 1983, many of these same people accepted the argument previously scorned and dismissed what they had earlier seen as one of the most important problems of U.S. defense policy. Of course much of this shift was disingenuous and can be explained by the imperatives of domestic politics, but I think it had other causes as well.[11] Once one shifts one's focus from the loss of American warheads to the remaining forces and their destructive ability, what had previously seemed to present the Russians with a dangerous opportunity seems just too dangerous a course of action to be taken.

This list of shifting views could easily be extended, but what is important is not that people change their minds or contradict themselves, but that the tensions are so severe and the choices so painful that a consistent position is hard to maintain. Awareness of the difficulties with one's views and the risks one's favored policies entail means that a person may be driven from them; lack of empirical evidence makes possible shifts in assumptions according to convenience. No one can be sure how stable the nuclear balance is or what kind of shocks it could withstand. The extent to which the mutual fear of all-out war inhibits adventurism similarly cannot be determined with certainty. The policy problems following from the choice of which of the interlocking elements one will focus on similarly cannot be completely resolved. Even if one starts with an understanding of the nuclear revolution, firm answers may be beyond our reach.

The difficulties in coming to grips with the implications of nuclear weapons are also revealed by the oddly selective nature of our nightmares. The line between vigilance and paranoia is always hard to draw in international politics, but what is noteworthy today is that while some of the hypothetical situations causing concern are even more farfetched than usual, others that could be seen as equally troublesome are ignored. Thus for years American leaders feared an attack on the land-based ICBM force but were not disturbed by the fact that the Russians could have easily wiped out those SLBMs which were in port.[12] Many analysts assume that the Russians could attack in Europe, but few fear a quick Sino-Soviet rapprochement and military cooperation against the West. The United States fears an attack by Russian submarines close to American coasts and is building missile-warning stations to cover the southern approaches to the country but is not concerned about Soviet "suitcase" bombs being brought into Washington, circumventing all radars and destroying the U.S. leadership without any warning. To worry about these dangers might be truly paranoid, but are they so much less likely than the risks we have chosen to focus on? When one faces a set of terribly unlikely but catastrophic contingencies, it is hard to find a sensible way to sort out which should be of concern. Thus analysts and decision-makers are susceptible to fads and the influence of accepted "ground rules" as to what they should worry about. The selection of problems is quite arbitrary.

A Spectrum of Escape Attempts

The nuclear revolution has produced not only tensions and inconsistencies, but also a variety of attempts to escape from the situation. I will discuss most of these briefly, and give extended attention only to those related to the central issues in the current strategic debate.[13]

First, some have urged that we regain the kind of security that was possible before 1945 by establishing an effective defense. Populations could be protected by the destruction of the other side's missiles (either on the ground or in the air before they reached their targets) and a system of civil defense. The goal may be desirable, but the fervor of the pleas that we try to reach it in the face of extensive evidence that it is simply unattainable attest to the difficulty of accepting the fact that our lives are in Soviet hands.

The psychological pressures are especially great for those who see the Russians as highly aggressive. For this view implies that there is a serious danger of war and that the United States may be forced to sacrifice important interests unless it is willing to fight. Although people who believe that the world is relatively safe and the Russians easy to deter do not like living with the possibility of destruction, they find the situation less of a strain. But if one sees the Soviets as strong, active, and terribly evil, it is very hard, both logically and psychologically, to tolerate the knowledge that one lives only at their sufferance. Thus it is not surprising that President Reagan strongly supports an anti-ballistic missile (ABM) system. At a press conference his view emerged with rare feeling: "To look down an endless future with both of us sitting here with these horrible missiles aimed at each other, and the only thing preventing a holocaust is just so long as no one pulls this trigger, this is unthinkable."[14] That the president's position is motivated by the felt need to escape from an intolerable situation is suggested by his rhetoric and confirmed by the absence of alternative explanations: the position has never been popular domestically; it is not favored by the armed services; the overwhelming majority of the scientific experts both in and out of government hold that the prospects for a successful ABM system are extremely low.

Arising at the other end of the political spectrum is another popular idea for escape, the recurring call for total nuclear disarmament. The insurmountable objections are well known, and I would just note that even if all nuclear weapons were destroyed, the knowledge of how to make them would remain. Doing away with the bombs would not do away with the problems of the nuclear era.

A third suggested escape route is less radical. It is simply to freeze current levels of weapons and technologies. I shall not

[55]

debate the merits of such proposals here, because what is relevant to my present purpose is that these plans recur and that they do not seem related to the details of existing or expected technologies and military balances. In other words, there seems to be something attractive about the notion of a freeze in the abstract; the idea does not derive all its appeal from an analysis of why current levels are preferable to others—just because the present is known does not mean it is better than the future. Furthermore, although a freeze might facilitate further steps in Soviet-American cooperation, it would directly affect only those aspects of our problems caused by changing technologies. As I noted earlier, this is not the heart of the matter. Thus it seems likely that much of the support for a freeze springs from the misplaced hope that it would undo many of the disturbing effects of the nuclear revolution.

Similarly, too much is often claimed for the idea of a conventional defense for Europe and a no-first-use policy. There might be advantages in such a posture, but it could not meet the danger that any large-scale fighting could escalate, a danger especially great because each side's conventional forces would be highly vulnerable to the other's tactical nuclear weapons. Thus even if NATO believed it could defend against a conventional attack, the risks of defense could produce the same effects that are said to flow from the existing force structure—the lack of credibility and the paralysis of political will.

Conventionalization: Explaining Nuclear Politics with Prenuclear Concepts

The most significant and pervasive escape attempt, one underpinning much of current U.S. doctrine, is what Hans Morgenthau called "conventionalization." This is the attempt to treat nuclear bombs as though they were conventional weapons, to apply the same ways of thinking to them that applied to armaments in the prenuclear era.[15] This view implies that there has not been a real nuclear revolution and indeed is psychologically attractive because it denies many of the new and disturbing elements—the fact that your fate rests in your adversary's hands, the split between what you threaten and what you would want to do, and the immorality of planning to kill millions of innocent civilians. It is intellectually attractive because it allows the analyst to use familiar concepts and apply ideas and arguments which have proven their utility over centuries of experience. But the denial of radical change cannot bring back the older world, and a policy that seeks escape in this way will make less and less sense as it becomes increasingly elaborate and precise.

Prenuclear thinking is revealed by statements which laid the foundation for the countervailing strategy, for example, Schlesinger's argument that the U.S. needs "implementable" threats and the position McNamara took in his famous 1962 Ann Arbor speech: "The U.S. has come to the conclusion that to the extent feasible, basic military strategy in a possible general war should be approached in much the same way that more conventional military operations have been regarded in the past. That is to say, principal military objectives, in the event of a nuclear war . . . should be the destruction of the enemy's military forces, not of his civilian population."[16] Paul Nitze makes similar arguments for the continuity between the nuclear and prenuclear eras: "The victor [in a nuclear war] will be in a position to issue orders to the loser and the loser will have to obey them or face complete chaos or extinction. The victor will then go on to organize what remains of the world as best he can."[17] The basic issue is brought out most clearly in a statement of Nitze's that epitomizes conventionalization:

It is a copybook principle in strategy that, in actual war, advantage tends to go to the side in a better position to raise the stakes by expanding the scope, duration or destructive intensity of the conflict. By the same token, at junctures of high conflict short of war, the side better able to cope with the potential consequences of raising the stakes has the advantage. The other side is the one under greater pressure to scramble for a peaceful way out. To have the advantage at the utmost level of violence helps at every lesser level.[18]

Nitze is correct: this is a copybook principle of strategy. But the copybook does not apply in the nuclear era; that is why it is not an exaggeration to speak of the nuclear revolution. Unless a state has first-strike capability, it is hard to see how having "the advantage at the utmost level of violence" helps. Indeed, it is even hard to tell what that means. It could mean being able to destroy the other side's strategic forces faster than he can destroy yours. Here World War III is pictured as a slow-motion counterforce war of attrition, a kind of long-range artillery duel. Of course if both sides accepted this picture, then the state believed better able to fight such a war would have an advantage in bargaining. But Nitze and others go further and imply that this ability brings advantages irrespective of beliefs, just as it did in the prenuclear age. Traditionally, gaining an advantage over the other side's forces made it impossible for the adversary to attack one's civilian assets. But now each side can protect its society only if the other side cooperates. The ability to wear down the other's missiles faster than he can destroy yours produces an advantage only at the end, when the other side is out of ammunition. Until that time, the side that is ahead is no more protected than the side that is behind.[19]

The copybook is now misleading: this point is a crucial one. To agree with Nitze's formulation is to accept the assumptions from which follow most of contemporary American nuclear policy. If force operates as it did in the past, if the established ways of thinking are still appropriate, then it follows that the best way to deter Soviet aggression is to construct a military posture which could do as good a job as possible of fighting a war if that should be necessary. But the fact that the attempt to proceed from prenuclear assumptions leads to a mass of contradictions indicates that this starting point is inadequate.

[58]

Escalation Dominance: Denying
the Adversary a Military Advantage

One major implication of conventionalization—and a theme that will reappear throughout this book—is the argument that a sufficient, and perhaps a necessary, condition for U.S. security is the establishment of escalation dominance, a condition which holds when the West is able to defeat Soviet aggression at all levels of violence, short of all-out war.[20] Thus, the theory goes, the ability to provide successful conventional defense would deter a conventional attack; matching capability at the theater nuclear level would deter the Soviets from using tactical nuclear forces; the ability to respond in kind to limited strategic attacks would cope with this kind of attack.[21] The West could then deny the USSR a military advantage from moves at any level of violence. The result, proponents of this view argue, would be that many of the dilemmas noted earlier would not arise: the United States would have implementable threats, it could protect itself and its allies at all but the highest levels of violence, and Soviet adventures could be defeated. But this escape route is also illusory. Even if the United States achieved these capabilities, they would not protect American cities in the event of all-out war, and that knowledge would inhibit the American actions at lower levels of violence.

Absolute and Relative Military Capabilities

A second implication of conventionalization is the need to stress relative, as opposed to absolute, capability. It is well known that when we deal with conventional weapons what matters is the comparison between two sides' armed forces on such dimensions as size, training, and equipment. Absolute capability, in the sense of size and associated characteristics of one state's army, tells one nothing because it is going to have to fight another army, and the question is which can win. But when the ultimate threat is the destruction of what each side values most and when inflicting damage on the opponent does not prevent him from doing likewise, then relative capability becomes less important than absolute.[22]

Despite this fact, most analysis of the strategic balance is carried out in a conventionalized framework. Many of the current assessments thus compare the number of missiles or warheads each side has or the number of hardened targets each can destroy, and many proposals call for equality between Soviet and American forces on these dimensions. At times it is implied that the Soviets might strike first if they thought doing so would destroy many more American warheads than it would consume Soviet bombs, thereby producing a better warhead ratio than that existing before the attack.[23] I cannot discuss all of the problems with these methods of measuring strength here,[24] but it should be noted that the implied metaphor of being in a race is fallacious. Not only does a race have a winner, but the logic and the measuring methods are derived from situations in which tanks, battleships, divisions, and other military units fought one another. Even then simple comparisons are misleading if they fail to consider such factors as training, tactics, and morale, or if they neglect the mission set for the military. For example, taking the offensive is usually more difficult than defending prepared positions, and a balance of forces more than adequate for the latter mission might not be sufficient for the former.[25] With strategic nuclear weapons, however, even a complex comparison between the two sides' forces misses the point. Because the targets of each side's strategic forces are not, or at least are not only, the other's strategic forces, knowing whether one is "ahead" or "behind" the other is not useful. One side could have more warheads or related capability than the other and still not have enough to menace the targets which were necessary for deterrence or for fighting a war; on the other hand, a state could have fewer military resources than its adversary and still have more than enough.

The same misplaced emphasis on relative capability appears

in comparisons of the extent to which each side can damage the other. One of the criteria that Secretary of Defense Melvin Laird held necessary for the essential equivalence of Soviet and American forces was: "Preventing the Soviet Union from gaining the ability to cause considerably greater urban/industrial destruction than the United States would in a nuclear war." General David Jones, then Air Force chief of staff, elaborated: "I believe that . . . relative post-attack recovery capability is a critical factor in measuring national capacities for waging and surviving nuclear war." As secretary of the Air Force, Harold Brown had earlier drawn the logical conclusion from this kind of reasoning: "even 25% Soviet casualities might not be enough for deterrence if U.S. casualities were disproportionately higher—if the Soviets thought they would be able to recover in some period of time while the U.S. would take three or four times as long, or would never recover, then the Soviets might not be deterred." As one analyst has put it, "Soviet civil defense programs plus population distribution asymmetries mean that . . . in a suicide pact, we would be 'deader.'" Nitze made a similar point nearly thirty years ago when talking about casualties and other forms of destruction which affect national power. He noted that one meaning of "winning" is "the comparison between the postwar position of the victor and the defeated" and argued that it is "of the utmost importance that the West maintain a sufficient margin of superior capability so that if general war occurred we could 'win' in [this] sense. The greater the margin (and the more clearly the Communists understand that we have a margin), the less likely it is that nuclear war will ever occur."[26]

In eras in which the targets of your forces were the forces which were attacking you, it made sense to ask which side was able to inflict more damage. And in cases such as strategic bombing in World War II, in which each side sought to reduce the other's ability to wage war by destroying its industrial base, it made sense to compare the rates at which each was being weakened. But under current circumstances it is hard to see why one would want to ask which side would suffer more. Statesmen do not go to war because they expect to inflict more damage than they will suffer; they do so when they think the expected utility of fighting is greater than that of remaining at peace. Comparing projected devastations is sensible only on the extreme assumption that the Russians are so highly motivated to expand that they would be willing to take enormous casualties in the expectation that, since they would recover faster than their adversaries, they would eventually dominate the world. Indeed, given the high levels of destruction entailed, it is hard to know who the "they" would be or what values they would stand for. (Russia ended up on the winning side in World War I, but this was little comfort to the tsar.) Thus Eisenhower told a Republican critic of his disarmament policy that "even assuming that we could emerge from a global war today as the acknowledged victor, there would be a destruction in the country [such] that there would be no possibility of our exercising a representative free government for, I would say, two decades at the minimum."[27]

Asking who would come out ahead in a nuclear war, either in terms of casualties or in terms of residual military and political power, assumes a zero-sum situation. Such an assumption made sense in eras when the costs of waging war were not prohibitive. The side that was ahead not only was better off than its adversary, but was likely to be better off than it would have been without a war. Now, however, even the side that is "ahead" of the other after a major war will be much worse off than it would have been had peace and the status quo been maintained. Again, the prenuclear ways of thinking have been carried over into a context in which they can only mislead us.

An interesting pattern in people's beliefs emerges on this point. Most of those who believe that nuclear weapons are weapons like earlier ones also believe that the Russians are highly aggressive; those who accept the nuclear revolution see the Soviet Union as less expansionist. To an extent, this consistency within each camp is suspicious because it should be possible to believe that nuclear weapons have revolutionized strategy and yet see the USSR as terribly aggressive or to believe that conventionalizing is appropriate and simultaneously hold a more benign view of Soviet intentions. But the beliefs have some logical connections because if one thinks that what is of primary importance is the overwhelming and mutual cost of war, then almost no country will be seen as hostile enough to trigger a conflagration. When one looks at it the other way around, the belief that the Russians are very aggressive implies that there is a chance they would employ force even at very high risk and cost. Although empirical evidence on this question is of course ambiguous and subject to dispute,[28] it is hard to argue that past Soviet behavior gives much reason to expect a willingness to run extreme costs in order to establish control of a postwar world.

In summary, many attempts have been made to escape from the dilemmas and paradoxes imposed by nuclear weapons. The most important is conventionalization, and this is the source of many of the ideas in the current countervailing strategy discussed in detail below. Most of these ideas would make sense were it not for the fact that throughout the bargaining before or during a war the civilizations of both sides would remain at risk. The attempt to fashion a strategy as though the nuclear revolution had not occurred can only make an already difficult situation even worse. The prenuclear guidelines are familiar and so provide psychological support and intellectual assistance, but they can no longer lead to coherent arguments and effective policies.

[3]

The Countervailing Strategy and
Its Areas of Incoherence

The problems discussed in the first two chapters indicate why
no nuclear strategy can be completely rational. But when one
attempts to escape from the nuclear revolution by conventionalizing, the situation is made even worse. Thus the countervailing strategy, starting as it does from these faulty assumptions, inevitably leads to incoherence and contradiction. But
before examining those areas of trouble I shall describe the
strategy in some detail.

WHEN DID THE COUNTERVAILING STRATEGY BECOME U.S. POLICY?

What period of time are we to analyze when discussing the
countervailing strategy? The name was coined by the Carter
administration, but President Reagan neither provided a new
one nor made many changes in substance. In terms of the projected strategic forces, the number of MX missiles has been cut
by the Reagan administration from 200 to 100, the B–1 bomber
has been added as an interim measure until the "Stealth"
bomber is ready, and, in a move which has attracted little attention but which could have serious consequences, a large force of
sea-launched strategic cruise missiles has been called for. In
terms of war planning, Reagan appears to put a bit more stress

on the possibility of a prolonged war and the need to be able to destroy Soviet missiles, and correspondingly to reduce the emphasis on flexibility, multiple options, and preparation for bargaining during the course of a war. But the differences here are not great.

A more noticeable Reagan departure has been the demand that the United States be able to "prevail" in a war.[1] Some have argued that this is to be taken seriously, as a part of an attempt not merely to contain, but to roll back Soviet influence throughout the world. American foreign policy has grown more ambitious, and so a more ambitious military strategy is needed to support it. This view seems to me to exaggerate the coherence of national policy and the significance of a few alarming phrases. Although it would not be surprising if the Soviets read more into them than is warranted (and if so, they may have influenced Soviet-American relations), there is no evidence that we are witnessing more than any administration's standard attempt to show that it has not fully adopted the policies of its discredited predecessor.

Although the term "countervailing strategy" dates from the late 1970s, many of the ideas and war plans it denotes can be traced back at least as far as the late 1950s and early 1960s. While public pronouncements have changed dramatically in the past twenty years—from "no cities" to "damage limitation" to "assured destruction" to multiple options and the countervailing strategy—targeting and the Single Integrated Operational Plan (SIOP) have been much more stable. Changes, though significant, have been evolutionary.[2] Many more targets have been added, much more flexibility has been introduced, and the priorities among kinds of targets have shifted.

The explanation for these changes, although fascinating and important, is not a central point here. One need only note that many of the basic ideas in current strategy have been embodied in U.S. targeting policy much longer than they have been part of declaratory policy. From the Truman era onward the United States has targeted Soviet military installations, and its plans have been based on "war fighting" as well as including strikes whose major effect, if not rationale, would be purely punitive. The goal never was to destroy only Soviet cities. Until recently, then, American war planning has more closely resembled Soviet doctrine (discussed below) than it has American declaratory policy. The changes in declaratory policy over the past five years have gone a long way toward closing the gap between what American officials said in public and what was in the SIOP. In passing, one may ask how the Soviets interpreted the discrepancy. It is likely that they saw it as further evidence of American hostility and duplicity.[3]

SUBSTANCE OF THE STRATEGY

If one looks beyond the difference in emphasis between Carter's administration and Reagan's, the countervailing strategy is seen to call for flexibility, counterforce of a variety of types, the ability to deny the Soviets an advantage from any military adventure, and the ability to menace what the Soviet leaders value. Driving it is a combination of conventionalization and fear that the stability-instability paradox could enable the Soviets to expand, especially if they are willing to run significant risks. In a world in which the threat to destroy the other's cities is no longer credible, the argument goes, fear of an all-out response can deter only an attack on one's homeland.[4] Indeed, it can deter only an all-out attack on one's homeland, since a massive response to a limited attack would only complete the destruction of one's own country. (Of course, credibility is not an all-or-none affair, and only a little may be required. See below, pp. 153–57.) To prevent intolerable Soviet moves, then, the United States needs a flexible military establishment that can allow it to match the variety of possible Soviet challenges with a variety of appropriate responses.[5]

Whatever the Soviets do, the United States should be able to maintain its military position, keep the conflict under control,

[66]

and communicate that its resolve is high. Some contingencies might call for a large strike against Soviet strategic forces. Others could require much more limited attacks, for example against Soviet submarine bases in response to a similar Soviet strike or a Soviet invasion of Iran. The latter aggression could also call for American nuclear strikes against Soviet forces in the area, thereby influencing the course of the local fighting. Since not all eventualities can be imagined ahead of time, there must be enough flexibility so that almost any combination of targets could be attacked.

The basic argument here is that the United States must design a posture that minimizes the gap between what it threatens in peacetime and what it would do in a war. In this way, it can develop "implementable options" that would enable it to deny the Soviets military advantage from any kind of adventure. Although defense in the sense of taking American cities out of hostage is not possible, defense in the sense of blocking the Soviets at lower levels of violence is. The Russians would be deterred, the advocates of this position believe, even if they doubted that the United States would devastate their country, because they could not gain anything from a war; they would not conquer any territory, they would end up losing more military resources and power than would their adversaries. If war became total, they would recover more slowly than the West and so could not expect to dominate what was left of the postwar world.

Were the United States in a position to do little other than resort to all-out war, the most obvious danger is that the Soviets would invade Western Europe. Following the logic of escalation dominance, the proponents of the countervailing strategy argue that the West should be able to meet the Soviet conventional threat on its own terms and, without moving to a higher level of violence, prevent the conquest. Similarly, the United States should have the ability to convince the Soviets that they could not conquer Europe in a war in which both sides used tactical nuclear weapons; it should also be able to fight a limited strate-

[67]

gic war in a way that would deplete Soviet military strength faster than it would deplete the West's. This logic applies to possible Soviet threats anywhere in the world. As Weinberger put it, "The Soviets have increased their capability so that . . . they are able to carry on simultaneous conflict in widely separated parts of the globe. It is necessary therefore for us to maintain our deterrent . . . capability of resisting aggression in more than one part of the globe."[6]

A subsidiary danger is that Soviet military advantage could be translated into political leverage without the actual use of force. The West could be coerced if others believed that it had no viable military options. As Zbigniew Brzezinski put it when talking about the specific problem of meeting one level of threat: "Should NATO be viewed as unwilling or unable to respond to threats of nuclear warfare confined to the European area . . . the opportunity for Soviet political pressures would be correspondingly enlarged." Even if the state of the Soviet military would not actually give the Russians an advantage in a war, the belief that it would is troublesome. Many officials echo W. I. Thomas's postulate: "If men define situations as real, they are real in their consequences." Thus it is frequently argued, as it was by Alexander Haig, that "perceptions of the military balance . . . affect the psychological attitude of both American and Soviet leaders, as they respond to events around the globe."[7] A statement of Harold Brown's is typical:

> The advantage to the Soviets of a possible lead in the primary measures of comparative capability is ill defined in terms of useful wartime capability. . . . But it might have some political value during peacetime or in a crisis. The perception of the United States–Soviet strategic balance has been and will be shifting away from that of U.S. advantage and becoming more favorable to the Soviets. Such perceptions can have an important effect.[8]

Soviet beliefs about the use of force are also crucial, and, according to the proponents of the countervailing strategy,

[68]

deepen the problems created by the stability-instability paradox. The Russians do not accept the distinction between defense and deterrence—they believe that the posture which can best deter any American use of force is the posture best designed to cope with that force if it should be used. This doctrine, it is argued, undermines a Western deterrent that stresses punishment rather than the ability to prevent the Soviets from reaching their goals. The Russians apparently do not view their ability to destroy American cities as an adequate deterrent against possible American adventures; they might similarly feel that an American countercity threat was an inadequate deterrent to their moves.

The primary aim of the countervailing strategy is deterrence. It is a war-fighting strategy in the sense of developing plans for how a variety of wars might be fought, but the objective is to show the Soviets that they cannot gain from a clash of arms and thereby restrain them. Deterrence is produced by counterforce, in a number of senses. Most generally, the countervailing strategy aims at meeting and countering the Soviets' forces—at stopping their troops and destroying other forms of Soviet military power. This was the dominant role of the military in the prenuclear age, and the attempt to return to it clearly points up the conventionalized nature of the thought behind the strategy. The strategy involves counterforce in more specific senses also. What has received most attention is the argument that in the event of war each side could and should concentrate much of its fire on the other side's strategic forces. Although neither side could wipe out the other's forces in a single blow, if the Russians believed that they could destroy many American missiles while maintaining a large force of their own, they might be tempted to strike, especially during a severe crisis, in the belief that they could prevail in a protracted nuclear war. If, by contrast, the Russians think that they would fall behind in such a counterforce war of attrition, they would not start one even if they were not deterred by the fear that meaningful limits could not be maintained.

[69]

One other possibility concerning strategic counterforce should be mentioned here, although it is explicitly denied by official U.S. statements: the launching of a partial disarming strike in response to a Soviet invasion of Europe. Of course American leaders could not be certain that such a strike would succeed, but a Russian leader, who would have to plan conservatively, might not be able to feel certain that it would not. The point of such a threat would be to restore the credibility of extended deterrence because the Russians would have real reason to fear a U.S. first strike. Adopting this posture would offer a much simpler rationale for current strategy than those which have been publicly put forward, and the idea has support within the Air Force. The obvious disadvantages of pursuing this goal are that the necessary capability is probably beyond the American reach and, if it were reached, would be hard to distinguish from a full first-strike capability.[9]

A different kind of counterforce is also seen as crucial for trying to deter or fight a war in Europe. Conventional forces would try to defeat the invading armies; tactical nuclear weapons—which would be employed if the Soviets introduced them or if the conventional efforts failed—would be used largely to provide maximum support for the NATO army; if strategic nuclear forces were used, they too would be concentrated on Soviet military targets in order to influence the battle in Europe and cripple Soviet military power. Thus a large proportion of the targets in the SIOP fall into the category known as Other (that is nonnuclear) Military Targets (OMT).[10] War-supporting industries would also be attacked to further sap the impetus behind the Soviet advance.

These two kinds of counterforce—the targeting of Soviet strategic forces and the tailoring of U.S. forces to defeat Soviet attacks on the ground—are both animated by the theory that deterrence is maximized if the adversary believes that, even discounting for the punishment involved in a war, he cannot gain the objectives he seeks or increase his relative military power. But the kinds of counterforce can be separated. One could, for example, endorse the second but see the first as a provocative, costly, and foolish denial of the efficacy of the threat to destroy Soviet cities in the most extreme contingencies. Alternatively, one could argue that the ability to prevent the Russians from prevailing in a protracted missile duel would also deter lesser provocations and so see the second kind of counterforce as unnecessary.

There are also some tensions between the two kinds of counterforce. Even though the U.S. stockpile of warheads is large, the number of military targets is larger still. The OMT list contains 20,000 targets; the Soviet strategic forces present at least 2,000 more;[11] U.S. warheads number approximately 10,000, several hundred of which would have to be retained for a residual force to hold Soviet urban and industrial targets in hostage. Furthermore, were the Soviets to strike first, many of these warheads would be destroyed. Thus to pursue one kind of counterforce would endanger the other. To keep ahead of the Soviets in a strategic counterforce war would severely limit the number of warheads available to support a war in Europe. Using up a lot of ammunition on OMT would reduce the American ability to destroy Soviet strategic forces. This choice is compounded by bureaucratic conflicts. The Air Force, the Strategic Air Command (SAC) in particular, has always stressed the importance of strategic bombing—which, indeed, is the central reason for its existence as an independent service. Emphasis on the importance of OMT and supporting a ground war in Europe or the Persian Gulf cuts against the grain and has been resisted. Nevertheless, despite these tensions, at the intellectual level the arguments for these two kinds of counterforce fit well together.

Another major strand of the countervailing strategy rejects counterforce, however. It stresses that while deterrence rests on being able to destroy what the Soviets value, it is a mistake to believe that their leaders are just like ours. That we place the highest value on our cities does not mean that they place the highest value on theirs. Instead, proponents of the strategy argue, the Soviets value the continued Communist control of the state, and so it is this we must threaten. Such a plan involves targeting the leadership and the cadres of the Communist party, KGB headquarters, Soviet internal security forces, and perhaps the army units along the Chinese borders ("opening the door to China"). Some proposals even advocate "ethnic targeting," which seeks to kill Great Russians but spare the Asian minorities so that the former would not control the post-war state.[12] The Soviets have to be convinced that no matter how the war ends in a military sense, their values and the Communist party would not prevail. This would deter them even if the expected loss of millions of civilians would not. (It should be noted that while the claim that the Soviet leaders place much greater value on continued Communist rule than they do on the lives of their citizens has some plausibility, there does not seem to be any evidence on this point. Instead, the conclusion seems to have been derived from general beliefs about the Soviet elite.)

INCOHERENCE OF THE STRATEGY

To reveal the areas of incoherence in the countervailing strategy requires close analysis of the official supporting statements. Three objections to this approach can be raised. First, because the doctrine has evolved over a number of years, some aspects of it may have been developed to meet circumstances that no longer apply. Thus some of the incoherence and contradiction may be best understood as incidental rather than as intrinsic to the enterprise. Second, various officials have somewhat divergent understandings of the strategy and the strategy itself is, to some degree, a product of divergent interests and analyses. Some of the internal incompatibilities can thus be explained not by the intellectual difficulties of trying to deal with the nuclear revolution in a conventionalized framework, but by the normal requirements of internal compromise. Third, some of the statements are disingenuous, designed to present justifications which are expected to gain greater public support than would a franker exposition of the strategy. The documents are always political and are often composed in haste; to read them years later for the assumptions and arguments may be to be misled.[13] Nevertheless, I think this approach is appropriate. Not only would it be hard to examine a doctrine without scrutinizing the rationales for it, but the problems raised by a reading of the documents involve more than wording. The arguments used fail to make sense because the underlying conceptualizations are badly flawed. One could not patch up the rough spots and express the same ideas with greater care or precision. Coherence and consistency can be purchased only at the price of abandoning the doctrine. Furthermore, the public pronouncements concerning the countervailing strategy seem to accord with actual war planning.

Four major points of incoherence will be treated here: the incompatibility of two major themes of the countervailing strategy (in that the one cannot meet the problem that the other says is facing the country); the ambiguity in what is meant by the claim that the United States has to be able to deny the Soviets victory; the desire for flexibility for its own sake; and the unjustified stress on the ability to carry out limited responses. Parts of these difficulties stem from the lack of a sensible view of war termination, a serious problem in a doctrine that claims to take the problem of fighting a war seriously. These instances of incoherence also reveal confusion or ambivalence about the requirements for, and even the meaning of, deterrence, a result of the fact that the countervailing strategy is largely built on conventionalization but cannot be entirely blind to the implications of the nuclear revolution.

Incompatible Strands in the Strategy

As we saw, one major strand of the countervailing strategy calls for varieties of counterforce while another calls for being able to destroy what the Russians value. Although individually these strands might make sense, they do not fit together. We should remind ourselves of the problem the strategy was designed to meet: in the words of James Schlesinger, "If the U.S. were to strike at the urban industrial base of the Soviet Union, the Soviet Union could and presumably would fire back, destroying the urban industrial base of the United States. Consequently, the Soviet Union, under those circumstances, might believe that the United States would be self-deterred from making use of its strategic forces. Thus, they might regard themselves as relatively risk-free if our deterrence doctrine, our targeting doctrine, were to stress only going against cities."[14] This sort of reasoning leads to the variety-of-counterforce strand of the countervailing strategy but undermines the other. The logic of this quotation would apply equally well if we substituted "leadership and political control" for "the industrial urban base of the Soviet Union." Threatening a strike at political control is the same as espousing the assured destruction position except that—a minor point in theory but a significant one in terms of operational planning—the targets to be destroyed would be different.

Under conditions of mutual vulnerability there is an inevitable trade-off between the credibility of a threat and the extent of punishment being threatened. It is the very fact that the Soviets value something so much—whether that thing be their cities or the control of their political system—that simultaneously makes the threat to destroy it so potent and so hard to believe. It is leaving what they value relatively untouched—and thus available to be destroyed later—that creates the incentives for the Russians to behave with restraint.[15] There would be no reason for the Russians to hold back once American forces had destroyed what they value most; therefore the United States would be deterred from destroying these targets. The threat to destroy Communist control of the state, then, does not meet the countervailing strategy's criterion for credibility; it is not an "implementable" threat. At best it could be carried out as a last resort, in retaliation for Soviet destruction of the United States.

But it is not clear whether such strikes, which place quite heavy demands on American weapons systems, could be carried out after several large nuclear exchanges.

Furthermore, neither of these strands in the strategy fits well with some of the arguments for flexibility. First, it is hard to calibrate attacks against leadership and political control finely enough, harder than with cities, which are stationary and easy to count. Not only are control targets more elusive; it is impossible to tell, even with good intelligence, how much damage has been done. At a certain point, political control might break down, but decision-makers (both American and Russian) could not know where and how close that point was. Second, to the extent that flexibility might call for the destruction of only a few targets as a demonstration of resolve, the basic axiom that American moves be militarily effective would be violated. These options would not contribute to defense; they would rely on the threat to exact greater punishment. While I will argue later that this is an effective means of bringing pressure to bear, it is not consistent with the premises of the countervailing strategy.

The links between the threat to destroy various kinds of targets and the reaching of political ends is thus unclear. Although the Carter administration said that "in our planning we have not ignored the problem of ending the war, nor would we ignore it in the event of a war,"[16] the countervailing strategy in fact does gloss over the question of whether American tactics could bring a war to at least a minimally successful conclusion. Why should certain kinds of nuclear strikes help terminate the war? What is the point of the exercise? Why should the threat to destroy certain targets dissuade the Russians from taking unacceptable actions? The strategy's failure to observe the distinction between deterrence by denial and deterrence by punishment is important here.[17] Deterrence by denial means deterring the adversary by convincing him that any attack will be thwarted, that he cannot win. Deterrence by punishment means convincing the adversary that it is not sensible to attack because doing so will lead to unacceptable costs. Although force may bring pressure through both channels, the analytic distinction is valuable for pointing out that there are two quite different ways in which the use or threat of force may have an effect and reminding us that any strategy should be clear on how its ends will be reached. In criticizing the effectiveness of deterrence by punishment and yet basing part of its plans on a form of this deterrence, current U.S. doctrine is incoherent. The strategy tries to move toward deterrence by denial, but cannot completely fail to recognize that the threat of punishment is inescapably central to superpower relations.

The Ambiguous Meaning of Denying an Enemy His Objectives

A similar question of the meaning of deterrence is also revealed in the ambiguity of many recent statements that deterrence requires the United States to have the forces necessary "to deny an enemy his objectives rather than to face him solely with the prospect of Pyrrhic victories."[18] Sometimes official spokesmen imply that what is required is deterrence by denial, that is, the ability to prevent the Soviets from gaining what they seek (for example, the conquest of Western Europe). Thus Harold Brown argues: "Our surest deterrent is our capability to deny gain from aggression by any measures of gain." Our strategy "makes clear to the Soviets that no course of aggression by them that led to the use of nuclear weapons . . . could lead to their victory by any reasonable definition of victory." Secretary Haig's position was similar: "War and, in particular, nuclear war can be deterred, but only if we are able to deny an aggressor military advantage from his action and thus ensure his awareness that he cannot prevail in any conflict with us."[19]

But this is not the only definition of what is required. A few pages after Brown's statement quoted at the beginning of the previous paragraph comes a quite different formulation: "For deterrence to operate successfully, our potential adversaries must be convinced that we possess sufficient military force so that if they were to start a course of action which could lead to war, they would be frustrated in their efforts to achieve their objective *or* suffer so much damage that they would gain nothing by their action." Many other statements are similar: "implicit in deterrence is the demonstrated ability and determination, should deterrence fail, to deny an aggressor its objectives *or* to retaliate so as to prevent it from gaining more than it would lose." On other occasions, deterrence through denial and deterrence through punishment are simply run together. Thus Brown argued, "our forces must be in a position to deny any meaningful objective to the Soviets *and* impose awesome costs in the process."[20]

Still a fourth formulation is common, one which directly contradicts the first one and implies a return to the deterrence-by-punishment position that underpins the scorned doctrine of assured destruction. Thus Secretary Brown told the Council on Foreign Relations: "Our basic strategy requires us to be able to inflict such damage on a potential adversary, that regardless of the circumstances, the prospect of that damage will preclude his attack on the United States, our allies, or our vital interests." He similarly argues that the United States needs to leave the enemy "no illusion of making any gain without offsetting losses." "Our countervailing strategy . . . tells the world that no potential adversary of the United States could ever conclude that the fruits of his aggression would be worth his own costs." Caspar Weinberger has also taken this position: "Our goal, our objective, and the only thing we are working for is to acquire a sufficient degree of strength at all levels, conventional and strategic, so that an attack upon us would be perceived correctly as causing a retaliation with a cost that would be found unacceptably big to the Soviets and therefore they would be deterred from making the attack."[21]

Thus while the countervailing strategy is always defended in terms of the need to convince a potential aggressor that he cannot win, the meaning of this idea shifts without reason. Sometimes both deterrence by denial and deterrence by punishment are seen as necessary, sometimes only the former (a major change from the logic of assured destruction), and sometimes the latter is seen as sufficient, even without the former. The variation has important implications for policy. To argue, for example, that the West must be able to "deny the Soviets a victory" in Europe would imply the need for forces that can physically repel an invasion. To "deny the Soviets the fruits of their victory" is a less demanding criterion and could be satisfied in a number of ways: the destruction of much of the Red Army, attacks on other sources of Soviet strength, or the demolition of the industrial base of Western Europe itself. This formulation recognizes that states are sensible enough to consider the costs of military action as well as the gains.

Although I do not have an exact count of types of statement, and one might not be meaningful, it is my impression that the dominant theme appears to be the need to ensure that the adversary does not think it can make "any gain without offsetting losses."[22] But this position has two implications that run counter to the rest of the countervailing strategy. First, it can mean that the United States does not need to be able to deny the Soviets a military advantage in a conflict. That is, it does not have to be able to keep them out of Western Europe, or ensure that they do not think that a war could enable them to pull ahead of the United States on various measures of counterforce capability. Second, destruction of Soviet cities and other values is such an "offsetting loss" that it is hard to see why the doctrine of assured destruction would fail to meet this criterion. Unless the Soviets emerged from a war with their social fabric intact, they could not enjoy the fruits of victory.

The other side of this coin is that if the ability to deny the Soviets their objectives is taken in the stronger sense of being able to prevent all Russian gains and protect American values, this end cannot be achieved without Soviet cooperation. Lacking an effective defense, the United States cannot prevent the Russians from destroying American society, as would be implied by a coherent doctrine of deterrence by denial.[23] Furthermore, even if the United States were able to deny the Soviets any direct military advantages from making certain moves—for example, to keep them from getting ahead in a silo-busting exchange—and prevent them from conquering Europe, it would not prevent them from coercing the West unless the West were willing to run a high risk of all-out war. The Soviets could advance even if the United States could match them at every level of violence if they convinced the Americans that fighting, even at low levels, was too costly and dangerous to be tolerated. We will return to this crucial point in chapter 5.

Flexibility as an End in Itself

Despite its superficial plausibility, the countervailing strategy's stress on the importance of flexibility similarly fails to come to grips with war termination or to result in careful arguments about how pressure can be brought to bear on the adversary without simultaneously putting as much pressure on the United States. The call for flexibility seeks to give the decision-maker a lot of choices in a crisis but is not supported by analysis of what effect the various options would have if they were implemented. Much of the explanation for this lack of analysis is that coherent answers are simply out of reach.

Flexibility is stressed in part because it is very hard to construct a convincing case for any of the proposed options. If particular choices made great sense—for instance, to attack a range of conventional military targets in Eastern Europe in response to a Soviet invasion of Western Europe or to hit a portion of second-level Soviet leadership in the event of an attack on the Persian Gulf—they could be specified in advance. The fact that statesmen cannot decide ahead of time what they would want to do is significant. Part of the reason they cannot is the difficulty in getting the president—almost any president—to take nuclear war seriously. What are the incentives for him to think through a painful choice that he is not likely to have to make? But part of the reason is that the problem is so difficult that one cannot develop a good answer to it. How can we tell what options will deter the Russians from proceeding and which would lead to escalation? What choices are most likely to terminate a war on acceptable terms?

If we could think this problem through to an intelligent conclusion, then we would have a much better idea of what we would want to do under specified conditions. Of course some factors would become known only as the crisis or war developed, but preliminary planning leading to tentative decisions could still be done on the basis of reasonable alternative assumptions about these factors. Instead of this, we seem to expect the president, or the person who becomes president as those higher on the list of succession are killed, to make an intelligent selection among options under unprecedented pressures—when we cannot make even tentative decisions in a calm peacetime atmosphere. This is implausible. Flexibility has become an end in itself and a substitute for the unattainable end of a strategy for terminating the war.

More specific problems also arise. First, the greater the amount of flexibility, the wider the range of choice a decision-maker will face in a crisis, thus increasing the burden on him. He will have to decide exactly how to respond, what kind of targets he wants to hit, and how hard he wants to hit them. Secretary Brown hints at the problem and his proposed solution: "What we plan to do, to the extent that it is feasible—there is a limit as to how many different options you can encompass and still have it be meaningful—we plan to put together targeting packages that are building blocks that can be tailored to a situation."[24] But there remains a conflict between keeping the decision problem manageable and making the packages numerous and small enough to be sure that the military will be able to carry out any mission the leaders might call for. The same difficulty is reflected at the technical level: increasing flexibility puts great pressures on C^{3}I systems since more information is needed and complex messages must be transmitted. The strategic forces themselves also need to be ready to shift from one set of targets to another, easy in principle but difficult in practice. Thus both mechanical systems and human decision-makers can be overwhelmed by flexibility.

The Ability to Make Limited Responses Is Not Enough

The incoherent rationale for flexibility is linked to the confusion in the arguments about the importance of being able to carry out limited options, especially limited nuclear strikes. These arguments gloss over two crucial and linked points. First, how is a limited war to be brought to a conclusion? The chairman of the Joint Chiefs of Staff argued that American strategic nuclear forces "must be flexible enough to ensure conflict termination at the lowest feasible level on terms acceptable to the United States, should deterrence fail."[25] But how can this task be accomplished? As long as the cities of both sides are vulnerable, why will it be the Russians rather than the Americans who make most of the concessions? It is hard to see how the ability to carry out limited options would produce this result.

The options will bring pressure to bear on the USSR only if they are carried out, and this raises the second difficulty. Although those who argue for flexibility are motivated by the belief that countercity strikes lack sufficient credibility, they ignore the impediments to the credibility of the threat on which they propose to rely. The problem was inadvertently illuminated by Secretary Brown: "In the decade ahead, we will have strategic retaliatory forces sufficient to deter Soviet attack, not only by the risk of escalation to massive destruction of cities and industry, but also by the *certainty of our ability* to destroy, on a more selective basis, a range of military and industrial targets and the seats of political control. This should surely deny the Soviety Union the advantages from embarking on a course of action that could lead to nuclear exchange."[26] Brown jumps from the claim that the United States will have the ability to carry out limited strikes to the claim that the threat to do so is sufficiently credible. This is the very ground on which he and

[81]

others criticize the assured destruction posture—the ability to undertake an action is only a necessary, not a sufficient, condition for credibility.

This problem, which is linked to that involved in the claim that we need "implementable" threats, touched on earlier, appears in slightly different forms in several other official statements. "It is our policy . . . to ensure that the Soviet leadership knows that if they chose some intermediate level of aggression, we *could*, by selective, large (but still less than maximum) nuclear attacks, exact an unacceptably high price in the things the Soviet leaders appear to value most." "Only if we have the ability to *respond realistically and effectively* to an attack at a variety of levels can we . . . have the confidence necessary to a credible deterrent." The ability to hit a range of targets "permits us to *respond credibly* to threats or actions by a nuclear opponent. No matter what the nature of the attack we would have the option to reply in a controlled and deliberate way, and to proportion our response to the nature and scale of the provocation." Deterrence "requires that we be *convincingly capable* of responding in such a way that [the Russians] would be denied their political and military objectives." "If our forces are *able*, with high confidence, to destroy [a range of military and nonmilitary targets], our deterrent should be *adequate to cope* with a wide variety of contingencies in as credible a fashion as nuclear weapons permit."[27]

The italic phrases highlight the incoherence in the reasoning. What does it mean to say a country's forces are "adequate to cope with a wide variety of contingencies"? In the prenuclear era there would be no difficulty with understanding this: it would mean that at reasonable cost the state could block others from reaching their objectives and, in so doing, would protect the state's values. But when the costs of blocking the other are very high, either in terms of the amount of blood and treasure directly consumed or in terms of the danger that the response will lead to intolerable escalation, then the ability to respond no longer means that the state's forces can cope with the contingencies. This is hinted at by Brown's closing phrase, "in as credible a fashion as nuclear weapons permit." The state's ability, "with high confidence, to destroy" a range of targets does not mean that the other side would have confidence that the state will destroy those targets. Brown speaks of "the certainty of our ability to destroy . . . a range of . . . targets." But what the United States seeks is to make the Russians certain of its response, or at least to make them place a high probability on it. The emphasis on the certainty of the American ability is misplaced since it fails to consider the fears that could inhibit the United States from acting on this ability. This difficulty is brought out nicely when Brown argues that deterrence requires the United States to "have the military capabilities necessary to exact the payment [from the adversary] (at a cost acceptable to ourselves), whether by denying our opponent his objectives, by charging him an excessive price for achieving them, or by some combination of the two."[28] The crucial question of how costs to ourselves will be limited, given the Soviet ability to deny the United States this objective, is only parenthetically acknowledged, not answered. Given Brown's perspective, indeed, no answer is possible.

Although a limited American response would be less likely to trigger the immediate destruction of American cities than would an all-out strike, the chance of an unacceptably painful Soviet reaction would still be considerable. The credibility of the American threat to retaliate is undermined less by the paucity of the kind of attacks which the United States could stage than by the vulnerability of American cities. Furthermore, the military effectiveness of the American response affects the credibility of the threat only marginally if at all. Even if U.S. forces can meet Secretary of State Edmund Muskie's requirement that they be able to deny the Soviets any "conceivable benefit from initiating the use of nuclear weapons," the threat to fight in the face of the Soviet ability to destroy U.S. cities is credible only to the extent that the Russian decision-makers believe that their American counterparts think that the war can be controlled and terminated successfully.[29]

If the ability to respond in a variety of ways were coupled

with the ability to protect oneself, as it was in many prenuclear situations, the logic of the countervailing strategy would make sense. Thus the objection of Colin Gray, whose perspective otherwise differs greatly from that employed here:

> No matter how flexible U.S. strategic employment planning may be, if it is not matched by some very significant ability actually to defend North America, it would have to amount, in practice, to suicide on the installment plan. Flexibility, *per se*, carries few advantages. Indeed, if the flexibility is very substantial and if the enemy agrees tacitly to a fairly slow pace of competitive escalation, it provides noteworthy time for the self-deterrence process to operate.[30]

There are only two ways out of this dilemma. One would be to develop the capability for defense, as Gray urges. But this step is not a part of the countervailing strategy, and few analysts think it is possible. The second, and less certain, way would be control the escalation process, to ensure both that the situation did not accidentally get out of hand and that the Russians did not steadily increase the level of destruction on purpose. But the countervailing strategy says little about how this could be done, just as it says little about war termination. As long as escalation is believed to be hard to control, parity or even superiority in the ability to carry out limited strikes does not make a great contribution to deterrence. On its own, that ability cannot lead to an escape from the central dilemmas discussed earlier, and so cannot enable us to cope with the problems which gave rise to the doctrine.

An important related problem is that while the countervailing strategy pays at least some attention to the credibility of threats, it completely ignores the need to make credible promises. Unless a war ends with one side running out of ammunition—a most unlikely contingency—some sort of negotiations will be required. Each side will have to believe not only that continued fighting is costly, but that peace is possible. This situation involves making and accepting promises for an immediate cease-fire and the belief that the other is not merely waiting for a favorable opportunity to renew the fighting. The ability to provide the necessary assurances is an indispensable part of war termination, a part no U.S. policy can afford to overlook.

[4]

Issues and Contradictions in the Countervailing Strategy

The previous chapter examined general characteristics of the countervailing strategy. Further problems are revealed when we look carefully at a number of specific issues that the strategy treats: the justification for the deployment of intermediate-range missiles in Europe; the practicality of the doctrine; the claims its proponents make about Soviet doctrine and outlook; the doctrine's premises about the possibilities of limited wars; and the argued need for counterforce parity, especially in combination with the claim that the "window of vulnerability" is not important. A close look at the rationales offered and the reasoning employed brings out a large number of contradictions within the doctrine. The analysis of official statements and assumptions required here must be detailed and intricate. One must follow out the implications of the doctrine and compare the arguments it has spawned in order to see that one cannot accept some of the premises and claims without rejecting others that are equally central. The contradictions that emerge are not the result of carelessness on the part of those who have formulated the doctrine, but rather arise from the impossibility of developing a consistent position if one uses concepts which cannot make sense of the nuclear world.

INTERMEDIATE NUCLEAR FORCES IN EUROPE

We start with the issue of Intermediate Nuclear Forces (INF). Although peripheral to much of the debate on general nuclear strategy, it reveals many of the difficulties which ensue when one tries to take the strategy's logic to its conclusion. (I do not mean to argue that logical clarity is either necessary or sufficient for a successful policy in this area.) The major objective of the United States in deploying these missiles in Europe is to reassure the Europeans[1] and show the Soviets that NATO is united. Much of the strategic rationale put forward may only be window dressing. It certainly does not explain many of the decisions that were reached, and what follows does not purport to be an account of those decisions.[2] The problem of presenting an official rationale for INF is especially great because some of the potential arguments for deployment are politically unacceptable to one or another of the NATO countries. For this reason the public pronouncements on the subject may disguise as much as they reveal. So the fact that the justifications offered contradict each other does not mean that INF should not be deployed. But the impossibility of developing a defensible rationale does reveal how hard it is to derive a sensible position from the assumptions of current U.S. strategic thinking. Furthermore, I think it is particularly significant that the most common justification for INF—the need to "couple" the American strategic forces to NATO—contradicts the basic logic behind the rest of the countervailing strategy.

One central confusion must be noted at the outset: is the INF deployment a response to strategic parity, or to the Soviet buildup in Europe and its most dramatic manifestation, the deployment of the SS-20 intermediate-range missile, or to both of these developments? Chancellor Helmut Schmidt's call for the West to take some action to bolster the defense of Europe was framed in terms of the Strategic Arms Limitation Talks' ratification of parity and the concomitant decreased credibility of the American promise to use its strategic forces. But most of the recent arguments have been couched in terms of the need to match the SS-20. It could also be argued, of course, that the two developments interact,[3] but one would have to show why the Soviet deployment creates specific problems which compound the stability-instability paradox.

[87]

To examine the twists and turns of the various arguments, it is necessary to take the several proposed purposes for INF deployment one at a time. The flimsiest argument is that of symmetry: because the Soviet Union can destroy NATO targets with forces based in the Soviet Union rather than in Eastern Europe, NATO needs a corresponding ability to reach into the Soviet Union. As President Reagan put it: "Now the only answer to these systems [SS-4, SS-5, SS-20] is a comparable threat to Soviet threats, to Soviet targets. In other words, a deterrent preventing the use of these Soviet weapons by the counter-threat of a like response against their own territory." Thus Brown argues: "with these new and more accurate weapons, the Soviets might make the mistaken judgment that they could threaten our allies without fear of retaliatory attacks on their territory."[4] (We should note that to focus on the high accuracy or other military qualities of the SS-20 implies that there is a significant chance that a nuclear war could be limited to Europe. That Brown denies this in the paragraph following the one quoted above only shows the difficulty in building a coherent rationale for the NATO policy.) Michael Howard is correct to label this sort of reasoning "politically naive to the point of absurdity."[5] There is no reason why the only, or even the best, deterrent against a menace should be a counterthreat which closely resembles it. It is particularly difficult to undertand why the shift in location of the Soviet missiles calls for a major Western reaction. Furthermore, even before the deployment of the SS-20, the Russians could have attacked Western Europe with missiles based inside the USSR (and indeed probably had earmarked some of their ICBMs for these targets[6]), and even without INF, NATO could strike into the Soviet Union from Europe by using F-111s based in England.

A more substantial justification for INF is the need to deny the Soviets escalation dominance and therefore to be able to match them in the ability to fight a tactical nuclear war in Europe. Without this capability, NATO could not credibly threaten to respond to a conventional attack (which it presumably could not defeat conventionally) by using nuclear weapons because such escalation would not reverse the course of the battle. Merely being able to hit a limited number of targets in Russia with NATO systems is not enough. As Brown put it: "NATO's strategy of flexible response has long been based on the ability to respond appropriately to any level of potential attack and to pose the risk of escalation to higher levels of conflict." An explanation given early in the Carter administration was similar: "It is precisely the military viability of NATO's response options, in the event [strategic] deterrence should fail, that enhances the deterrent."[7]

The problems with the escalation dominance position are discussed elsewhere in this book. The point here is that this argument fits neither with the kind of deployment proposed for INF nor with other more frequently offered rationales. It does not meet criteria for fighting a war because, given the political inhibitions against moving the missiles off their bases, they will be highly vulnerable to a first strike, perhaps even one with conventional weapons. From a military standpoint, the American missile-launching submarines now earmarked for NATO are more effective. INF would have higher chances of survival if based on ships and submarines, and the rejection of sea-based systems largely on nonmilitary grounds (the felt need for the new weapons to be "visible"[8]—which in the current political climate is a mixed blessing) further underscores the inconsistency of the American position.

What is most central, however, is that the whole line of argument that it is necessary to rectify the imbalance in theater nuclear weapons undermines the two linked cornerstones of Western policy: nuclear war cannot be limited to Europe, and the Russians are deterred by the perception that Europe and the United States cannot be separated. Why is parity in tactical nuclear forces (TNF) needed unless NATO is planning to be able to fight a nuclear war which would not involve the superpowers' strategic forces? To the argument that the United States knows such a war could not be kept limited but needs the war-fighting ability to deter the Soviets who might believe the contrary, the obvious response is that the NATO effort reinforces rather than undermines this putative Soviet perception. Putting so much effort into correcting what are seen as deficiencies in the theater balance can only lead to the inference that NATO is preparing for a limited war. Indeed, many Europeans have drawn this conclusion, and have opposed matching the SS-20 with an equal number of NATO INF lest the Soviets be led to believe that the American strategic forces might not be used in a NATO–USSR war. Out of their own fears of coercion, the Soviets have also seen the Western deployment and rationale as implying preparation for a limited war and have sought deterrence by rejecting this possibility. In the words of one Soviet spokesman: "If the U.S. would use these missiles in Europe against the Soviet Union, it is not logical to believe we will retaliate only against targets in Europe. Let me tell you, if some of your experts think this, then they are foolish."[9]

The Coupling of NATO and American Strategic Forces

Most American arguments agree with the Soviet position. They deny that war-fighting is the main role for INF and claim that a war in which they were used could not be confined to Europe. Indeed, the main purpose of the new weapons would be to make such limitation less likely, to link European and American fates more tightly. As a State Department official, Richard Burt, put it: "The expansion of the Soviet ICBM force, coupled with Moscow's advantage in conventional forces, brought to reality a prospect Europe had long faced—the possibility that a nuclear conflict might be limited to Europe." INF is an appropriate response, according to Burt, because the Soviets know that these weapons, if used or attacked, would trigger the U.S. strategic force. Thus he argues that "the U.S. took this step [of advocating INF] in the full knowledge that the Soviet Union would most likely respond to an attack on its homeland by U.S. systems in Europe with an attack on the U.S." Former Secretary of State Kissinger agrees: the deployment of INF will "increase the risk to America, not to Europe; logically the public demonstrations against them should be on the American side of the Atlantic." President Reagan's official statement drives home the point: "The essence of United States nuclear strategy is that no aggressor should believe that the use of nuclear weapons in Europe could reasonably be limited to Europe."[10]

Following out this line of argument, however, leads to contradictions and implausible assertions. Even within its own framework, the conclusions cannot be accepted without denying some of the premises. To begin with, the whole claim made for the importance of coupling is inconsistent with the escalation-dominance, counterforce, and defense-by-denial themes of the countervailing strategy. If one believes that the Soviets can be deterred only by the threat of actions which would prevent them from making any gains, how can one argue that the function of INF is not to show the Russians that an invasion of Europe could not succeed, but to convince them that the result of the attempt would be to trigger U.S. strategic forces? After all, the supposed incredibility of this latter threat was the main impetus for the countervailing strategy.

Most analysts agree on the need to tie the United States and Europe together, but the arguments for INF in this connection make little sense. To start with, is coupling best conceived in terms of the operations and implications of weapons? As Michael Howard argues, "The United States is 'coupled' to Europe, not by one delivery system rather than another, but by a vast web of military installations and personnel, to say nothing of the innumerable economic, social and financial links that tie us together into a single coherent system."[11] If the United States values Europe enough to run high risks to keep it free, the Russians will be deterred. If it does not, the Russians could blackmail the United States into withdrawing regardless of the forces it had on the Continent.

One can reply that political ties are insufficient for coupling in light of what it would cost the United States to come to Europe's assistance. The deployment of NATO nuclear forces is needed as a form of commitment; once on the scene they would automatically involve the United States in any fighting that took place. Ground troops, although a necessary part of this deterrent, are insufficient because they are not tightly enough linked to strategic nuclear weapons. NATO also needs TNF because any Soviet attack would lead to their use if they were not themselves struck by a Soviet blow. In either event the American strategic force would be triggered; the Russians, understanding this, would have to choose between starting World War III or leaving Europe alone.

According to one line of argument, the weapons are important mainly because they will draw Soviet nuclear fire. The onus not only of starting the war but also of using nuclear weapons first[12] would then fall on the Soviets. Thus Kissinger's justification for INF: "the Soviet Union could not risk attacking Europe with conventional weapons without destroying our intermediate-range missiles also, lest they devastate Soviet command centers in a retaliatory blow. And it could not seek to destroy the missiles in Europe while leaving our strategic arsenal in America unimpaired for a possible strike against Soviet ICBMs."[13] Current TNF cannot menace command centers in the USSR; American submarines assigned for NATO use, which can do so, are invulnerable and so would not be attacked. Even if one ignores the point that this argument rests partly on the fact that INF would both be vulnerable and decrease Soviet security, one must realize that it implies that the Russians would have to attack INF in the event of war, but could launch a conventional attack which spared NATO's current tactical nuclear weapons.[14] (It should be noted that, to the extent that this logic is correct, it would hold whether or not the Soviets deployed SS-20s. The American "zero-option" arms-control proposal should accordingly be unacceptable to the West because it would eliminate NATO's INF.[15]) But the logic of the argument is weak. The Soviets have valuable forces in

Eastern Europe and could hardly afford to leave NATO TNF unscathed and able to attack them. The targets in the USSR may be more lucrative, but are not the ones presently menaced, including the Red Army, crucial to the success of a Soviet attack? If so, the Russians would have to attack TNF as the war started, and thus they provide the same coupling that would be produced by INF.[16]

An alternative form of the coupling argument is that while the USSR might launch a conventional attack against NATO even if INF were deployed, the West would be able to use these weapons in response. But if firing INF would lead to a world war—and this is what coupling means—and the result of such a war would be the destruction of American society, why is the threat to use these forces credible? If American leaders thought a war in Europe would lead to world war, they would feel enormous pressure to find a peaceful solution in a crisis, even if doing so meant sacrificing other values. This was the effect of coupling in 1938. France was pledged to Czechoslovakia and Britain was tied to France. Prime Minister Neville Chamberlain therefore knew that a German invasion of Czechoslovakia meant an Anglo-German war. Since this prospect was unacceptable, Britain had to bring pressure to bear on the Czechs to get them to concede. The British were not willing to face war in 1938; if American leaders are not, INF will become a means for transmitting pressure from Europe to the United States; if they are, their range does not matter.[17]

Two replies are possible. The first is that, although an American INF response would not be credible if the decision could be made upon calm reflection, the physical placement of the weapons ensures that there would be little choice. As Kissinger put it, "The proposed deployment . . . would create the imperative of a certain automaticity in the response."[18] But where does this automaticity come from? Firing the weapons still requires a presidential decision. The choice might be "use them or lose them," but the latter would be preferable to a world war. Indeed losing the weapons would be a significant cost only if one

[93]

were thinking of the military balance in Europe, and such a concern implies that the war would be limited to the Continent, which contradicts the basic idea of coupling. Nevertheless, there is something to Kissinger's claim: the very fact that these weapons are vulnerable decreases the probability that the war could be kept limited. But not only does this line of argument apply to the current TNF as well as to the proposed force; also its logic is similar to that of assured destruction. It stresses the importance of commitment, relies on irrationality, and denies the need to match a wide range of Soviet provocations with an equal range of Western options.

The second possible reply is that the threat of using these weapons is more credible than the threat to fire ICBMs because although the latter action would certainly lead to the destruction of American society, the former holds open at least the possibility that the war could be kept limited. Furthermore, the United States would find it easier to use INF than to employ the NATO-designated SLBMs for the same mission because the latter, being part of the U.S. strategic force, are more likely to trigger Soviet escalation than is the former. By using INF, then, NATO can signal that it is trying to preserve limits. Were it certain that the limits would hold, this approach would lead to decoupling. But since such certainty is impossible and using the weapons would create a great danger of escalation, that danger is avoided. Existing TNF are not adequate on this score. Because they cannot reach into the Soviet Union, the Russians might be confident that their use would not lead to a wider war. The use of INF would generate just the right amount of risk— not so much that the Russians could be confident that the Americans would not use their strategic forces, but enough so that the Russians would be deterred.

This line of argument is alluring, but there are two objections to it. First, it is overprecise in claiming that the level of risks falls into the narrow band just described. With all the enormous uncertainties involved, it is hard to argue that the Russians would believe that the Americans would consider the SLBMs too dangerous to employ but would not be similarly inhibited from using INF. Second, existing NATO tactical weapons would indeed do as well as INF in providing the necessary risk. They would even be a bit better than the proposed systems just because most of them do not reach into the Soviet Union and so the credibility of NATO's using them would be a bit higher. But since the risk of escalation would still be very great, all but the boldest or most desperate of adversaries would be deterred from starting an adventure which would lead to their use.

Coupling and the Logic of the Countervailing Strategy

The most significant aspect of these arguments for the coupling function performed by INF is not that they are defective or can be applied as well to shorter-range systems, but that they deny the need for escalation dominance. Thus, Secretary Weinberger argues that deterrence flows from "the clear Soviet understanding of the certainty that a conventional/nuclear war in Europe risks engagement of the central nuclear systems of the United States."[19] I agree with this line of reasoning and will develop it further in the next chapter, but it shows that the whole argument for the importance and possibility of coupling rests on assumptions and mechanisms very different from those underlying most of the countervailing strategy. Coupling contradicts the need to deny the Soviets any gains, to develop "implementable options," and to close the gap between what threats the United States makes in peacetime and what it would do in the event deterrence fails. The whole point of coupling is to show the Russians that they cannot be sure that the United States will not respond in a way which could lead to mutual destruction. But, as the proponents of the countervailing strategy stress in their critique of assured destruction, it is hard to make such threats credible. Thus coupling and credibility are inherently in tension with each other, and this tension is magnified by a view that stresses the need for measures to be militarily effective in order for threats to employ them to be believable. The arguments about coupling just discussed are plausible because they move away from the assumptions of the countervailing strategy and instead rest on the sensible belief that the Russians can be convinced that moves which might be militarily advantageous are much too risky to be worth taking. But if one accepts the idea that coupling deters the Soviets in Europe, how can one reject the idea that coupling similarly deters limited Soviet attacks on U.S. strategic forces? If the USSR would not dare attack Europe without simultaneously seeking to destroy NATO's nuclear forces, or would not dare attack the latter without simultaneously striking U.S. strategic forces, how could it dare attack only some military targets in the United States, leaving the others unscathed? The ties between parts of the American forces are even tighter than those between the United States and Europe, the links between limited and all-out use of American strategic weapons are closer and more automatic than those between NATO and American forces, the chance of maintaining control is even less with a limited strategic attack on the United States than with a tactical nuclear conflict in Europe. Far from being consistent with the countervailing strategy, as Brown insists,[20] the main rationale for INF deployment contradicts it.

PRACTICALITY OF THE COUNTERVAILING STRATEGY

Another issue that reveals the incoherence of the countervailing strategy is the impracticality of the measures called for. The pressures to escape from the nuclear revolution are so intense that people have been driven to a doctrine which could not be implemented. Taken seriously, the countervailing strategy is an incredibly demanding one.

Number of Warheads Required

To start with, the United States probably does not have a sufficient number of accurate and easily controllable warheads to hit all the targets whose destruction the strategy posits as necessary. To hit silos and Soviet leadership targets alone would require 4,200 accurate warheads.[21] If it is believed that deterrence requires also putting at risk the Russians' conventional military targets (OMT), which would influence the course of a war in Europe, the United States would need much larger forces, although some of these targets could be destroyed by less accurate warheads. In addition, some munitions must be withheld to hold hostage urban and industrial targets. Although the United States has about 10,000 warheads in the strategic force, proponents of the countervailing strategy argue that only the ICBMs are suited for many of the most important counterforce missions, and this force contains about 2,150 warheads, only the most recent models of which (numbering 1,650) are reported to be large and accurate enough to menace strongly protected targets such as silos and underground command posts.[22] The deployment of the MX and the Trident II would at least partly close this gap—and would threaten the bulk of Russia's current strategic forces—but much would depend on future Soviet programs. Furthermore, the U.S. forces must be prepared to hit all these targets not only in response to a Soviet conventional attack on Europe, but also after receiving a Soviet first strike. In the latter case, of course, the valuable MX and Minuteman III warheads would not be available.

Before examining the other requirements that put the countervailing strategy out of reach, we should note two ways in which the necessity for so many warheads contradicts other aspects of U.S. policy. First, it flies in the face of the American proposals for deep cuts in strategic forces. Sharply reducing the number of warheads available, even if the Soviets made comparable cuts, would not leave a sufficient number to destroy their leadership and OMT, especially if the United States needed to keep a city-busting force in reserve. Under some conditions of technology, mutual reductions make sense as a means of decreasing the incentives for either side to launch a first strike against the other's strategic forces. But if the United

States is seeking deterrence through the ability to destroy other targets, then it may not be able to afford to decrease its forces even if the Russians do.

Requirement of such large numbers of warheads also clashes with other aspects of the strategy in that it is hard to reconcile with the stress on the importance of ICBMs. Even if a hundred MX are deployed, less than one third of the U.S. warheads will be on land-based missiles. This implies that SLBMs and bombers can be used to attack many of the targets called for in the countervailing strategy. But if they can, then the ICBMs are not necessary to carry out most of the missions, and it is not clear why one should be especially concerned about the vulnerability of this part of the force.

Command, Control, Communications, and Intelligence

The arguments in the two previous paragraphs can perhaps be dismissed by the rebuttal that the Strategic Arms Reduction Talks proposals and worries about ICBM vulnerability are largely matters of domestic politics—political propaganda, to put it more bluntly. There is much to this, although it still leaves us with the problem that the United States lacks sufficient warheads to implement the countervailing strategy. But this shortfall is probably the least of the barriers to the strategy's practicality. Not only warheads are needed, but also attack assessment capability, retargeting ability, enduring command, control, and communications (C^3) facilities, accurate and immediate intelligence on the status and disposition of Soviet forces, and continuing political communications with the Soviet Union which could facilitate restraint and make possible termination of the war. The U.S. force does not meet these requirements now, will not meet them even if all programs curently proposed are implemented, and, given anticipated technology, is never likely to meet them.

The obstacles are enormous. To hit the top Soviet leaders requires knowing where they are. A large number of shelters exist, and we have no indication that the United States could tell which ones housed the key individuals. Furthermore, the shelters may be too well protected to be destroyed. If the United States wanted to threaten not the lives of the Politburo members, but the Communist party's control of the country, it could try to hit KGB headquarters, party cadres, and internal security facilities. But while the locations of the relevant buildings and camps are known, the people probably would not be there during a crisis, especially since they have been told that they are prime targets.

Hitting OMT presents similar difficulties. Bases and barracks are stationary, but the forces move. Unlike the targets just mentioned, these military units are large and thus, in principle, amenable to detection. But locating them would require reconnaisance, either by aircraft or by satellites, and the survival of these systems in a conflict is highly questionable. Even if the satellites survived and the United States had many stations that could receive the information they were transmitting, the number of stations that control satellites is very small and if their capability were lost, the satellites would soon drift out of position.[23] Perhaps these systems would all continue to function, either because the Soviets spared them (which they might not be able to do even if they tried) or because all links were sufficiently protected and redundant, but it is hard to see how a sensible strategy could be based on this assumption.

Similarly, the C^3 systems are very vulnerable. Desmond Ball and others have documented this problem well and only a few points need be noted here.[24] Although the president has a flying command post, it does not seem likely that he could reach it if he waited for radar warning of an attack. He would thus have to decide whether to have himself evacuated at an earlier stage of the crisis. This would be a major political step and although of course no firm evidence is possible, it seems unlikely that any president would take it. If a president did not, the problem would be especially great: with Washington destroyed and most of the political leaders dead, how would the person who succeeded to the presidency know that he was commander-in-chief? How well informed would he be about the war plans? How would he communicate his orders to the military?[25] Even if he reached the surviving military leaders, would the communication links from them to the forces remain intact?

These problems are much greater under countervailing strategy than under assured destruction because the load of signals imposed on the system is much greater. Complex instructions have to be given and the leadership has to be kept informed about what missions have been carried out and how the battles are progressing. Although this is easy to say, it is terribly difficult to do. It would be hard enough for commanders to locate their own forces, let alone keep track of where the enemy troops were, which targets had been destroyed, and what restraints the enemy was obeying. An enormous amount of information would have to be gathered, collected, analyzed, and conveyed to the military commanders and national leaders during battles of unprecedented lethality and complexity. Decisions would have to be transmitted quickly and accurately all the way down the line, although just finding the people in charge would be a major task. Even if we leave aside the difficulties of reaching careful decisions under pressures we can hardly imagine, there is no reason to believe that the purely technical problems can be overcome.

Endurance of the Forces

All the C³I systems must work, furthermore, not only for a few hours, but throughout an "enduring" or "protracted" war. Official statements are not clear on exactly how long a period it is thought this would be. According to one source, in 1978 the goal was eight hours,[26] a length of time not sufficient to fight the kind of war recent formulations envisage. The flying command post could stay in the air for seventy-two hours at the most (although of course either enemy fire or the huge amount of dust put into the atmosphere by the nuclear explosions might bring it down much sooner), but even this is too short a time for a war that would include supporting the battle in Europe. Perhaps the C³I systems could be reconstituted to function over a longer period, but this seems little more than a hope.

Of course the ability to fight a prolonged war calls for weapons systems as well as C³I to survive. This requirement is relatively easy to meet with that portion of the sea-based force which is out of port when the war starts, but it is much harder to maintain the ICBMs and bombers. Those of the latter that survived a Soviet first strike and the attrition of the air defenses would have to find undamaged airfields, get new supplies of bombs, and rendezvous with surviving tankers if they were to be used in a protracted war. ICBMs would be even less likely to survive repeated strikes (assuming the Russian intelligence facilities continued to function). Their openness to attack is particularly significant because much of the concern about Minuteman vulnerability has been based on the argument that ICBMs are particularly well suited for war-fighting and the maintenance of deterrence during a war. But these missions call for more than surviving an initial strike; they require the systems to be available throughout the war. So it is particularly odd that the Reagan administration was willing to spend billions of dollars to deploy the MX in a dense pack configuration which, while it would have provided significant protection against destruction in a single strike, could have survived only for a few hours if the Russians launched multiple attacks that the United States was not able to disrupt. The current plan to put the MX in Minuteman silos, of course, is even less consistent with the notion of a protracted nuclear war.

One additional practical point which is easy to lose sight of is that if the war is to be kept controlled, all Western forces (and the Chinese, too, if they are involved) will have to cooperate. But while there is some technical coordination among the American, British, and French strategic forces, there is no evidence that the latter two would refrain from hitting Soviet cities. Indeed, given their number and characteristics, these weapons would not have much use unless aimed at the most important countervalue targets. One of the major points of McNamara's Ann Arbor speech and the parallel private NATO briefings was to try to convince Britain and France that independent Western nuclear forces were incompatible with the hope of fighting a restrained nuclear war. No one, now or then, has tried to refute this claim, but the United States has built a doctrine that simply ignores the problem. Even if no other obstacles were present, this one alone would be enough to undermine the policy.

Replies and Summary

To these arguments for the impracticality of the countervailing strategy, two lines of rebuttal are possible. First, it can be acknowledged that many aspects of the strategy are now beyond reach; only after several years of increased spending could the United States implement them. The documents set forth the requirements and the goals, they do not pretend to describe current capabilities.[27] But it is far from clear that the requirements can ever be met, even at high levels of spending. There is no reason to believe that detailed information and precise control can ever be achieved, especially if the adversary does not make great efforts to cooperate. A second possible reply is that even if the chance of American systems being able to function over a prolonged period of war is slight, the United States should plan in these terms in order to do as well as possible should war occur. But if the primary goal is deterrence, as U.S. leaders have said, then the impracticality of the doctrine is more of a problem. If Washington says that the Soviets will be deterred only if U.S. forces can perform missions which in fact they cannot—and which Russian leaders think their American counterparts know cannot be carried out—then Soviet adventurism might be encouraged. More likely, but still troublesome, would be the excessive caution induced in American decisionmakers by the realization that their forces cannot meet what they set out as the requirements for deterrence. The United States is wounding itself by opening an enormous gap between what it says it needs and what it can do.

In summary, the countervailing strategy ignores Clausewitz's dictum "Everything in war is very simple, but the simplest thing is difficult." Maintaining control of American forces, locating Soviet targets, and keeping track of what is happening are easy in the abstract, but terribly difficult under actual wartime conditions. Intra-war deterrence—and that is what much of the countervailing strategy calls for—requires that both sides carefully coordinate their military moves with their political strategies, communicate their positions clearly, and accurately judge the other side's posture. These things proved impossible to do in the comparatively calm and simple conflict in Vietnam;[28] the problems would be much greater in the unprecedented and catastrophic context of a limited nuclear war. Furthermore, everything would have to be done right the first time it was tried. The impracticality of the strategy is one of the reasons why many of the Air Force officers who would have to fight the war oppose it.[29] Indeed all these problems are so great that if academics, rather than policy-makers, had come up with this doctrine I think the latter would be justified in saying that it was typical "ivory-tower" thinking, which simply assumed away all the practical difficulties in favor of dealing with abstractions. That otherwise practical men and women have been driven to such a doctrine is yet another sign of the extreme pressures generated by the felt need to escape from the nuclear revolution.

SOVIET DOCTRINE

One of the main criticisms of the theory of assured destruction is that it assumed that the Russians saw the world the same way that the Americans—or rather, American proponents of assured destruction—did. The doctrine might be appropriate if the Russians had a similar outlook. But they do not, and so an alternative strategy is necessary, one built with an eye not only toward abstract principles of deterrence, but, according to the advocates of the countervailing strategy, also toward the beliefs and military doctrine specific to the Soviet Union. The Russian doctrine, which denies at least some aspects of the nuclear revolution, calls for an American response that is at least partly conventionalized.

While I strongly agree with the basic argument that it is important to take the other side's perspective into account, in fact this is not the foundation for most of the countervailing strategy. In many important areas Soviet doctrine is treated as irrelevant; at other points the strategy's proponents provide no evidence; in still other areas, the strategy, far from being built around Soviet perceptions, contradicts them in ways that lead the United States to create imaginary problems and propose unworkable solutions.

First, it is often said that the United States would not need a counterforce doctrine if the Soviet Union did not have it, that the United States needs multiple nuclear options because the Russians have them, and that it needs to be able to fight a protracted nuclear war only because the Russians see this as a real possibility. But these claims misattribute the causes of the Amercian strategy.[30] Once the assumptions on which the countervailing strategy rests are accepted, most of its prescriptions follow even if the Russians believe in MAD as a policy. The desire for flexibility, nuclear counterforce, and "implementable" options which are thought to be militarily effective are not linked to Soviet doctrine.

To put the problem another way, why would the American threats be more credible if the Soviets believed in assured destruction? If the United States needs to be able to do more than deny the Russians a Pyrrhic victory, would this not be the case whatever doctrine they adopted? Indeed the perception that the Soviets believed in MAD could lead to even greater pressures to find ways of meeting the Soviet threat to Europe and other

[104]

areas on their own terms because it would highlight the stability-instability paradox. The countervailing strategy tries to
bolster the credibility of extended deterrence by threatening the
limited use of strategic nuclear weapons if the USSR should
invade Western Europe. But this is not possible if the Soviets
convince the West that they do not think such wars are possible. From this perspective it is not surprising either that the
Soviets have rejected the idea of limited strategic war (a point to
which I will return) or that, according to a close student of the
Schlesinger doctrine, many of those who in the early 1970s
argued that the United States needed more flexibility "hoped
that the Soviet Union would eventually introduce limited-use
concepts into her own strategy."[31]

The historical record confirms what logic suggests: that it is
the vulnerability of U.S. cities more than perceptions of Soviet
doctrine which is responsible for the countervailing strategy.
The seeds of this strategic view extend far back, long before
there was any attention to what the Russians thought. Some of
the ideas elaborated in current strategy (for example, attacking
Soviet nuclear facilities and OMT) were central to U.S. war
plans even when the Russian nuclear forces were small. And as
parity became first a major worry and then a reality, more aspects of the strategy were adopted, both under McNamara and,
a decade later, under Schlesinger. But even the latter plans
were made before there was concern that the Soviet military
doctrine stressed war-fighting. Although both worry about Soviet doctrine and the countervailing strategy developed over
time, the latter preceded the former more than it followed it.

The argument that it is not cities but Soviet leadership and
political control that we must hold in hostage is, of course,
rooted in beliefs about the Soviet outlook. But although this
claim is plausible, where is the evidence to support it? Would
the Soviet leaders really consider waging a war if they expected,
say, 100 million casualties, but thought that the Communist
party would rule the ruins? To look at the other side of this
coin, even if it is Communist rule that Soviet leaders value, do

they believe that it would vanish with the destruction of the party apparatus and internal security forces? They might be that cynical, but they could also believe that the party is supported by the population and would regenerate after a war, especially if the cities were left intact. In the late 1940s, some American analysts believed that nuclear attacks would lead to revolts in Russia, a conclusion questioned by the Harmon Report, the first systematic examination of what nuclear bombing would do to the USSR.[32] Now, as then, what is needed is evidence as to what outcome the Russians expect.

Is the Countervailing Strategy Compatible with Soviet Doctrine?

More important, although advocates of the countervailing strategy claim it is based on Soviet doctrine, in fact the two are widely discrepant. Although the strategy's proponents accuse its critics of "mirror imaging" the Soviets (believing that the Soviets see the world as they do), they commit the same error. The policy of flexibility and intra-war deterrence, far from being designed "with the Soviets in mind,"[33] is incompatible with the Russian perspective. This is not to say that Soviet doctrine is that of assured destruction. The Soviets do not seem to see advantages in mutual vulnerability. Rather, if war comes they want to limit damage to themselves and do as well militarily as possible. They prefer deterrence by denial to deterrence by punishment, and many of their views fit the pattern of conventionalization discussed earlier. As one would expect of doctrine set by military professionals, it takes war seriously. But what is crucial is that the nuclear war the Russians are thinking of is one without restraint. Whether they struck out of the blue, pre-empted in a crisis, or responded to the use of nuclear weapons by the West, they would seek the best military solution to the problem. While they would not target American population per se, write Benjamin Lambeth and Kevin Lewis, "nothing in Soviet thinking remotely approximates the Western idea of sparing enemy cities for 'intrawar bargaining.' . . . [T]he Soviet conception of the initial period of war envisages rapid, intense, and simultaneous nuclear strikes against very large numbers of countermilitary and countervalue aim points in combination." Although of course one cannot be certain that the Soviets' position would not change in a crisis, John Erickson points to the links to broader political issues that make their views quite deeply-rooted: "The Soviet rejection of the idea of limited nuclear war is axiomatic, based as it is on the political notion that political objectives—not the performance of particular weapons—decree the essence or scope of war: it follows, therefore, that if American objectives are 'unlimited' in the sense of regaining military superiority and escalation dominance over the USSR, then any war operations cannot be 'limited,' whatever the technicalities of the weaponry involved."[34]

Soviet doctrine thus undermines the countervailing strategy in several ways. First, the need felt by Secretary Brown "to convince [the Russians] that they could not win such a [limited nuclear] war" is illusory.[35] (I do not know what the Russians make of the American claim that it is they and not the Americans who are most interested in the idea of limited strategic war. I doubt if they see it as an innocent error.) Similarly, the United States does not have to worry that the USSR might employ coercion based on its supposedly superior ability to wage such a war. Western leaders might deter themselves on the basis of such a fear, but it is Washington's belief that is dangerous, not Moscow's. Third, the elaborate American plans for keeping a nuclear war limited, far from responding to Soviet doctrine, are vitiated by it. Unless the Russians change their outlook, the United States cannot preserve its society in a nuclear war even if the practical obstacles discussed earlier are overcome. The U.S. doctrine rests on rules the Russians simply show no sign of accepting.

Will the Russians See Only Countervailing Threats as Credible?

The proponents of the countervailing strategy can concede that the Russians reject the idea of limited nuclear war, but still argue that Soviet military doctrine is troublesome. Since the Soviets equate deterrence with the ability to fight a war as effectively as possible, the argument runs, American threats that do not fit this frame of reference will not be judged credible. The Soviets believe that their own security can be guaranteed only by the ability to rebuff American advances; they will therefore think they can advance unless the United States has a similar capability. But this reasoning is superficial. First, it is not clear that the Soviet doctrine has any relevance to deterrence at all. Instead, it may be only a discussion of what should be done if deterrence fails. The best analogy may be to an insurance policy—something one has to minimize damage if the worst should occur but which in no way inclines one to behave recklessly.

To the extent that Soviet doctrine has other significance, it sets the requirements for deterrence very high. It implies that a policy which involves much risk of armed conflict must be supported by a military posture which could fight a war to an acceptable conclusion. The Russians know that significant unilateral damage limitation is still beyond their reach, however. Their society and political power could therefore be saved in a war only if the other side were to permit it. But the Russians do not place much faith in the possibility of keeping a war—even a conventional one—limited under current conditions, perhaps in part because of their aversion to relying on restraint on the part of their adversaries.[36] Thus the Soviets are likely to be self-deterred. A final point is linked to the previous one: even though the Russians—like the proponents of the countervailing strategy—do not accept the idea that mutual assured destruction is a desirable state of affairs, they understand that it exists and creates a situation in which pressing the other side too hard can bring disaster. As one expert put it, "there is nothing to suggest that the Soviet leaders think that a general nuclear war would be anything other than catastrophic, for the victors as well as the vanquished." Harold Brown concluded after first saying that American strategy must be tailored to his distorted view of the Soviet outlook: "All this does not mean that the Soviets are unaware of the destruction a nuclear war would bring to the Soviet Union; in fact, they are explicit on that point. Nor does this mean that we cannot deter, for clearly we can and we do."[37] The Russians accept the reality of MAD as a situation even though they reject it as a desirable policy.[38]

CAN NUCLEAR WARS BE KEPT LIMITED?

The question of whether nuclear war can be kept limited is relevant not only to the compatibility of American and Soviet doctrines, but also to the validity and coherence of the American doctrine in its own right. Of course, the lack of empirical evidence and the role of doctrine in shaping behavior limit the degree to which any reliable answer is possible. Nevertheless, one can expect a greater degree of consistency in response than one finds in current U.S. doctrine. The proponents of the countervailing strategy usually argue, quite sensibly, that one cannot be sure whether limits would be possible. Escalation, either planned or inadvertent, could occur, but might not. Rare was the unequivocal claim made by Secretary of Defense Schlesinger:

I believe . . . if we were to maintain continued communications with the Soviet leaders during the war, and if we were to describe precisely and meticulously the limited nature of our actions, including the desire to avoid attacking their urban-industrial base, that in spite of whatever one says historically in advance that everything must go all out, when the existential circumstances arise, political leaders on both sides will be under powerful pressure to continue to be sensible.[39]

More frequent are notes of greater uncertainty. Thus Brown argued:

In adopting and implementing this policy, we have no more illusions than our predecessors that a nuclear war could be closely and surgically controlled. There are, of course, great uncertainties about what would happen if nuclear weapons were ever again used. . . . I am not at all persuaded that what started as a demonstration, or even a tightly controlled use of the strategic forces for larger purposes, could be kept from escalating to a full-scale thermonuclear exchange. But all of us have to recognize, equally, that . . . it should be in everyone's interest to minimize the probability of the most destructive escalation and halt the exchange before it reached catastrophic proportions. Furthermore, we cannot count on others seeing the prospects of a nuclear exchange in the same light we do.[40]

Before examining the odd aspects of arguments such as Brown's, we should note one which makes sense: no one can guarantee that nuclear weapons will not be used, and, if they are, it is in the interest of both sides to keep the war limited (although each could want to use the chance of escalation as means of extracting concessions from the other). As Colin Gray argues, even though the chances of efforts at limitation succeeding are "slim," they should be made: "The stakes are so high that almost any way of improving our (and their) prospects of retaining central control of forces by responsible political authorities has to be worth pursuing."[41] This position sees U.S. policy not in terms of deterrence, but of insurance, albeit of doubtful efficacy.

Most aspects of the administration's arguments go further, however, and claim that convincing the Russians that the United States can fight a limited war strongly enhances deterrence and may even be necessary for it. The first odd thing about this position is the implication that the United States needs this ability because the Russians are thinking of limited nuclear wars—when in fact such ideas are antithetical to their doctrine. The central problem, however, is raised by the common claim that "there is no contradiction between this focus [on what to do if a war were to break out]. . . . and a judgment that escalation of a 'limited' to an 'all-out' nuclear war is likely. Indeed, this focus helps us achieve deterrence and peace, by insuring that our ability to retaliate is fully credible."[42] But there is a contradiction. The threat of a limited response can be more credible than that of all-out war only if the Russians believe that American leaders believe that escalation can be avoided. To the extent that one thinks such a progression inevitable, one will view a limited response as merely a way of delaying the time of suicide. What is crucial for the added credibility that the ability to carry out limited strikes brings is not the Russians' beliefs about whether nuclear war can be kept limited, but their beliefs about what the American decision-makers think about this question. Indeed, deterrence would be maximized if the Russians thought control was impossible, but believed that the United States thought it was relatively easy. In that case, they would not only refrain from using or threatening limited strikes, but would also find American threats to do so in response to Soviet nonnuclear provocation quite credible, since the United States would see such a response as carrying only manageable risks. Furthermore, the Russians would see these strikes as leading to disaster, and thus would pay almost any price to avoid triggering them. But official spokesmen have undercut deterrence by taking the opposite position: they incorrectly impute to the Russians the belief that nuclear war could be kept limited while confessing that they themselves have grave doubts. Thus Brown argued that in the event of a limited nuclear exchange, "avoiding escalation to mutual destruction is not likely."[43] This means that the problem with the coupling of NATO and American forces discussed above reappears in a slightly different guise. You cannot argue that the threat to destroy the other's cities is incredible because your own cities would be attacked and then claim much greater credibility for threats whose implementation you admit would soon produce the same result.

COUNTERFORCE PARITY AND ICBM VULNERABILITY

Other problems are revealed by the argument that the United States needs to match the Soviet Union in strategic counterforce

[111]

capability. Even greater contradictions arise if one follows the Scowcroft Commission in combining this position with the argument that ICBM vulnerability is not a major concern as long as timing problems prevent the Russians from simultaneously attacking all components of the U.S. strategic force. (I should note at the start that it probably is not wise to take the commission's report too seriously in terms of kinds of arguments I am making here. It is a highly political document, drafted to create a consensus. As such it succeeded brilliantly, much better than most observers, myself included, had thought possible. By the same token, some of the commission's claims may be disingenuous. But it still is important to consider the implications which should follow from the belief that the ICBMs do not offer a "window of vulnerability." What appears at first to be a technical point is actually built on assumptions relevant to many aspects of the countervailing strategy.)

The arguments for counterforce parity are common and constitute one of the main justifications for the MX. As the Scowcroft Commission put it: "A one-sided strategic condition in which the Soviet Union could effectively destroy the whole range of strategic targets in the United States, but we could not effectively destroy a similar range of targets in the Soviet Union, would be extremely unstable over the long run. Such a situation could tempt the Soviets, in a crisis, to feel they could successfully threaten or even undertake conventional or limited nuclear aggression in the hope that the United States would lack a fully effective response."[44]

Here several points made earlier are relevant and need only be mentioned. We are not in a race, and asking who is ahead on hard-target kill capability is particularly foolish because each side's warheads should be matched against the other's targets, not against each other. Furthermore, counterforce parity cannot be the only criterion for an adequate strategic force because it would be met by mutual first-strike capability, and no one seriously seeks this instability. (A few statements indicate that the United States has considered seeking it, however. Edward

[112]

Rowny, chief START negotiator, regrets that the United States is "behind in a number of destabilizing weapons systems" and the commander-in-chief of SAC argues that "a silo-based Peacekeeper will resolve this fundamental and destabilizing imbalance by placing at risk the Soviets' newest and most lethal assets."[45] But most U.S. officials have seen that matching a destabilizing posture is not a wise objective.)

The official position yields silly implications because it equates the concerns arising from three very different kinds of situations. First, there is the perceived need to stay even with, if not ahead of, the Soviet Union in a counterforce war of attrition. Although factors not caught in the simple comparison between American and Soviet forces, such as who struck first and the effectiveness of C³I systems, would be extremely important, in this context one could sensibly argue for parity. But as I have argued elsewhere in this book the model of nuclear war as a long-range artillery duel in which the side that runs out of ammunition loses is hard to accept. Indeed, the main justifications for counterforce parity do not rely on this rationale. The second concern contained within the call for extensive counterforce capability is that the United States might not have enough warheads remaining after a Soviet first strike to menace all the targets which must be held at risk: Soviet leadership and political control, OMT, and remaining strategic targets. But counterforce parity is not a measure of adequacy in this context. The number of accurate warheads the United States needs is determined by the number of Soviet targets, not the number of Soviet warheads. Furthermore the necessary American forces must survive a Soviet strike, and so what is crucial is the vulnerability of the American missiles as well as the accuracy of the warheads. Needless to say, the deployment of MX in silos will not help solve this problem.

The third concern is that the United States would have to launch a first strategic nuclear strike in response to a Soviet attack on Europe. Here the Scowcroft Commission makes two arguments, one implausible and the other serious, though flawed. First, it claims that "ICBMs are especially effective in deterring

Soviet threats of massive conventional or limited nuclear attacks, because they could most credibly respond promptly and controllably against specific military targets and thereby promptly disrupt an attack on us to our allies."[46] To the extent that attacks on OMT and leadership were required, speed would not be necessary and cruise missiles, if not gravity bombs, should be sufficient even if we accept the notion that strategic nuclear forces might be used as long-range fire-power to support a war in Europe. Second, if the targets were Soviet strategic forces and the idea was that the United States would have Type II deterrence, as the commission implies in some parts of its presentation,[47] the argument is sensible, but raises obvious questions. Even with the MX, could the United States knock out most of the Soviet forces? As we will note below, the combination of planned American forces indeed might be able to reach this objective if the Soviets failed to build new weapons systems, but is it reasonable to expect them not to do so? Furthermore, could the United States establish Type II deterrence without gaining a first-strike capability? Theoretically, the answer is clearly yes, but given the tendency of military planners to calculate conservatively, the answer is probably no.[48]

This problem cannot be disposed of—as the Scrowcroft Commission does—by arguing that MX "would provide a means of controlled limited attack on hardened targets but not a sufficient number of warheads to be able to attack all hardened Soviet ICBMs, much less all of the many command posts and other hardened targets in the Soviet Union."[49] It is not clear how this would deter the Soviets. Such an American strike would leave U.S. cities vulnerable. Of course, the strike would destroy some things the Russians valued, but neither the MX nor parity with the Soviets in counterforce capability is necessary for this task. Rather, the United States needs enough warheads to hit the required targets, which in the commission's formulation are not linked to Soviet counterforce capability. Furthermore, the case for the MX in this regard could be made only if it were shown that the U.S. reply had to be prompt. But

[114]

such promptness would make sense only if the American strike were a disarming one, which the commission says it would not be.

In explaining the need for the MX, Weinberger says that without prompt retaliatory capability, "for the crucial first few hours of a nuclear conflict, the bulk of [the Soviet] ICBM force and supporting command and control structure would remain largely immune to U.S. retaliation."[50] But it is not clear why the first few hours should be so crucial. What could the Russians do to affect the course of the war decisively in the few hours before U.S. bombers, cruise missiles, and SLBMs struck?

In summary, the claim that the United States needs parity with the Soviet Union in counterforce capability (or in prompt counterforce capability) confuses three separate objectives. It is particularly important to distinguish between the goal of being able to destroy much of Russia's strategic forces on a first strike in order to bolster extended deterrence and the need to have enough warheads to hit desired targets after a Soviet strike.

The dismissal of the current "window of vulnerability," which at first seems unrelated to the justifications for parity I have been discussing, actually undercuts them and indeed contradicts many of the assumptions underlying the countervailing strategy. The Scowcroft Commission argues that as long as the Russians cannot hit the entire American force with short-warning SLBMs, the vulnerability of land-based ICBMs is not crucial. The reason is the well-known timing problem: if the Soviets were to time their attack so that SLBMs hit bomber bases just as the missiles aimed at the ICBM fields were detected, the United States would have twenty minutes after the bombs landed on the airfields in which to launch its missiles. On the other hand, if the Russians chose to avoid this danger and have their missiles land simultaneously on the bomber bases and ICBM fields, the United States would have twenty minutes' warning time in which the bombers could escape. This argument makes sense, and the only apparent question is why many people had previously rejected it. But what is of interest here are the implications of this position, implications the commission did not draw.

First, this claim contradicts two of the three rationales for counterforce parity. While it leaves untouched (and may even reinforce) the argument that the United States needs to be able to launch a disarming strike in the face of a Soviet attack on Europe, it implicitly denies that a counterforce war of attrition is a serious possibility and that the United States needs a lot of warheads to cover OMT and political control targets after a Soviet first strike, two concerns which imply that ICBMs have characteristics that make them especially valuable. They are accurate and can respond promptly, and, unlike the SLBM, one missile can be fired without making the others more vulnerable (one SLBM launching may reveal the location of the submarine). Typical is a recent statement by Secretary of State George Shultz, which accompanied his endorsement of the Scowcroft report:

> If the Soviets can strike effectively at our land-based ICBMs while our land-based deterrent does not have comparable capability, the Soviets might believe that they have a significant advantage in a crucial dimension of the strategic balance; they could seek to gain political leverage by a threat of nuclear blackmail. Without arguing the question of whether the Soviets are prepared to launch a nuclear first strike, such a crucial imbalance in the strategic capabilities could well make them bolder in a regional conflict or in a major crisis.[51]

But to downgrade the significance of the window of vulnerability is to deny the significance of the ICBMs' special characteristics. If their survival were necessary for deterrence, then there would be a danger that the Russians would attack them even though the SLBMs at sea were invulnerable and the bombers on alert could escape. To argue that the Russians would not carry out such an attack is to claim that the SLBMs and bombers are adequate to carry out whatever missions are needed for deterrence against a massive counterforce strike.

[116]

I have no trouble with the latter argument, but the proponents of the countervailing strategy should. If one says that the ICBMs are needed only for a first strike (either full-scale or limited—although, contrary to the Scowcroft Commission's claim, it is hard to see why ICBMs should be particularly valuable in the latter contingency), then this is the equivalent of saying that the United States does not need to worry about having a great deal of prompt second-strike hard-target kill capability. To put the point the other way, if one were concerned about showing the Soviets that the United States could stay ahead in a counterforce war of attrition or could promptly destroy many Soviet hard targets even after the Soviets had struck first, then one would have to worry about the window of vulnerability. The survival of bombers and SLBMs could not compensate for the destruction of American ICBMs because the latter would be needed to threaten the targets whose peril, the doctrine says, would deter the Russians. For example, if a slow-motion war of attrition were a real possibility, would not the Soviets be tempted to attack American ICBMs because doing so would give them an enormous advantage in this contest? To reply that the Russians would be deterred by the damage the United States could inflict with bombers and SLBMs is to deny that a war of attrition is worth worrying about. Similarly, to argue that the Russians would not attack American ICBMs if they could not simultaneously destroy the other strategic forces is to acknowledge that ICBM warheads are not needed after a Soviet first-strike for such missions as attacking Soviet forces in Europe or destroying the Communist party's political control of the Soviet Union.

Finally, if the window of vulnerability is not a matter for much concern, why does the United States have to worry about Soviet counterforce capability? If one accepts the argument that this capability cannot be used for a massive strike against American strategic forces, then what contingencies do appear as dangerous? One could worry about an attack against other hardened targets, such as C^3, but these are few in number. A

[117]

reduction in the size of the Soviet heavy missile force would not go far to protect them. Yet much of U.S. arms-control policy and many of the rationales for the deployment of the MX (repeated, among other places, in the Scowcroft Commission report) are based on the objective of moving the Russians away from their large counterforce missiles.

In summary, the supposed need for parity in counterforce capability involves three contingencies leading to quite different lines of argument and force requirements. The problem can be approached sensibly only if one breaks these down and specifies which is of concern. Furthermore, at least two of the arguments are incompatible with the dismissal of the current problem of American ICBM vulnerability. Indeed if one accepts the Scowcroft Commission's logic on this point, it is hard to accept most of the countervailing strategy. The fear of a war of attrition, the requirement of denying the Soviets any military advantage, the worry about Soviet counterforce capability—all should be put aside. Of course that has not been done, even by those who served on the commission or endorsed its report. The obvious inference is that the new stand on ICBM vulnerability springs from the knowledge that political and technical constraints make it impossible to find an invulnerable basing system for the MX, coupled with the belief that the MX is needed to demonstrate American will. At bottom, the commission was largely addressing problems of American image and domestic politics, not of strategic posture. But it is nevertheless interesting that the end result of its efforts was to undercut much of the rationale for current policy.

SPECIFIC CONTRADICTIONS IN
THE COUNTERVAILING STRATEGY

Because the countervailing strategy is not based on an appreciation of the nuclear revolution and yet the vulnerability of American and Soviet societies is too glaring to be ignored, a number of specific contradictions arise. This is inevitable; given the requirements that the strategy establishes for deterrence, parts of the argument cannot but contradict other parts. Many of the problems spring from the difficulty of managing the increased tension between conflict and cooperation that the nuclear revolution has generated, a difficulty with which the countervailing strategy is particularly ill equipped to cope because of its conventionalized intellectual framework.

Should Soviet Leadership be Attacked?

The first contradiction of this type arises in the strategy's plans for dealing with the adversary's C³I facilities during a war. On the one hand, the countervailing strategy supplies an important rationale for hitting Soviet command and control facilities, but, on the other hand, it also indicates why the United States should not do so. To the extent that the doctrine seeks to limit American casualties by means of attacks on Soviet strategic forces, it points to the need to attack such targets. Because C³I is a major factor in multipling force effectiveness, degrading it is of great military value. Indeed it is at least possible that either side could escape retaliation if it launched an all-out first strike at the other's C³ facilities. (The United States is probably much more vulnerable in this respect than is the USSR.) Thus it is not surprising that the Reagan administration is apparently placing increased stress on attacking these facilities.[52] But this impulse conflicts with the need to spare C³ if the war is to remain limited. If the United States destroyed the Soviet leadership, with whom could it make peace? (One should not imagine that any new regime which formed would be pro-Western. Instead, it would probably be strongly nationalist and would still control nuclear weapons.) Secretary Brown briefly acknowledged this problem when he noted that although the United States wants the ability to take these targets under fire, it might not attack them.[53] But this merely avoids the conflict. Under what conditions would the United States want to destroy the leadership and under what conditions would it want it to survive?

[119]

The other side of this coin is that American forces could not wage the sort of war envisaged by the countervailing strategy without C^{3}I facilities. I noted above that it is unlikely that they could survive without Russian cooperation. But to assume that the Russians would disregard the strong military incentives to attack them is very odd. It is possible at least to imagine a war in which each side hit military targets (and perhaps intelligence systems) but avoided C^3 (although of course their co-location would pose great problems)—and such a war would be an exquisite illustration of the extent to which nuclear weapons have heightened the imperatives for both conflict and cooperation—but both the political and the technical obstacles would be enormous. It is clear that the countervailing strategy has not developed a coherent view of how to manage the contradictory pressures that the question of attacks on leadership generates; there is no reason to believe it can ever do so.

Civil Defense and Civilian Casualties

A related contradiction appears in the countervailing strategy's attitude toward Soviet civilian casualties during a war. The logic of the position implies approval of the Soviet civil defense program as it applies to the general population. If the Soviet leaders value their civilians highly, then the United States would need to spare them in order to keep the war limited. And if the Soviets do not, as one strand of current doctrine holds, then attacking them does little good. Indeed the desire to avoid killing innocent civilians led the U.S. military to argue against targeting "cities per se" as early as 1950.[54] In the same vein, many analysts applaud the improved accuracy of delivery systems not only because they make Soviet strategic weapons vulnerable, but because they allow American forces to destroy targets within cities without destroying the cities. Furthermore, officials say that the United States is not planning to retarget its forces to take account of possible evacuation of the cities.[55] This all makes sense, but it also implies that American strategists should favor effective Soviet civil defense. In fact, however, the dominant analysis sees Soviet civil defense planning as both an indication of aggressiveness and a threat to the efficacy of American retaliatory strikes. This attitude would be appropriate for proponents of assured destruction, but most of these people doubt that the Soviet plans would work. That supporters of the countervailing strategy think that the Russian program is efficacious owes a lot to their general image of the Soviet Union; that they think it is a menace betrays a visceral understanding of the limitations of their strategic assumptions.

A third contradiction arises because of the related need to keep American casualties down. Even if one assumes Soviet restraint, fallout patterns are such that, according to William Perry, under secretary of defense for research and engineering in the Carter administration, a full Soviet counterforce attack would cause "very substantial incidental deaths in the civilian population" and could essentially be regarded as "a counter-value attack."[56] Most calculations are conservative in assuming that the Soviets would attack only SAC bases and not be concerned with the possibility that the B–52s would be dispersed to civilian airfields, many of which are located near large cities. But could a Soviet planner take the risk of sparing these facilities? There would be strong military incentives for the United States to use these airfields, as it did during the Cuban missile crisis.[57] Indeed one argument in favor of the B–1 is that it can operate off six thousand runways compared to the two hundred which B–52s can utilize.[58] The United States, then, does not seem willing to trade military advantage for encouraging Soviet restraint and is making plans that will make such restraint even less likely.

On the other hand, to the extent that American analysts fear that the Soviets might initiate a limited nuclear war by attacking U.S. strategic forces and sparing cities, an appropriate response would be to ensure that such an attack would have to be close to all-out. If this is the objective, the fact that the B-1 can be dispersed to so many airfields increases its value. But if the

United States were to be consistent, it would place more of its strategic forces near population centers, making it impossible for the Soviets to attack them without removing all restraints on the American response. Instead, the MX is proposed for places far from cities. Because it and the Minuteman III are particularly capable of destroying hardened Soviet targets, American leaders worry about an attack which might be limited to those systems. American ICBM deployment thus seems designed to make possible the kind of Soviet attack which is feared.

The Strategy's Image of the Soviet Union and Soviet Security

A fourth contradiction involves the general image of the Soviet Union underlying the strategy. The proponents of the countervailing strategy see the Russians as quite aggressive, highly motivated to expand, and willing to take significant risks to reach that end. This, they argue, is the explanation for the Soviet arms buildup over the last fifteen years. But they seem to expect these same Soviets to fail to respond to the American plans, to allow the United States to alter the strategic balance and defeat the scheme. If the Russians are as driven to increase their influence as this view suggests, is it not likely that they will divert the resources necessary to match the American buildup? Three responses are possible. First, it can be argued that the Soviet economy is so stressed that military spending cannot be increased. Second, the Soviet programs may be completely unresponsive to American ones—the reasons for their posture may derive entirely from a rigid plan or internal imperatives. Third, even if the Russians do increase their forces, the American buildup may be sufficient to deprive them of significant political leverage; that is, the American systems may be effective enough so that Soviet matching efforts will not have great impact. But while there is something to these responses, they seem insufficient to account for the puzzling juxtaposition of fear of the Russians and expectations that they will be passive.

In their belief that the requirements for deterrence are very demanding, American officials may have drawn themselves into a fifth contradiction. Although they claim that U.S. policy is compatible with Soviet security, they may have defined security and the capabilities necessary for it in such a fashion as to make this largely untrue. Harold Brown has stated that the United States needs to be able to put at least one warhead on each hardened Soviet target.[59] This presumably is on a second strike, and thus there is a need for many more warheads which could be used in a first strike. Similarly, Weinberger says that it is vital "to ensure nuclear force parity, across the full range of plausible nuclear war-fighting scenarios, with the Soviet Union."[60] Since these would include strikes initiated by the Soviet Union under conditions most favorable to it, the requirement probably cannot be met without denying the Russians a similar ability. If the American leaders feel they need not only to stay even with the Soviets in a counterforce war but also to be able to hit large numbers of command and control bunkers, the number of hard-target killers needed would be even more threatening. These weapons, coupled with a fairly impressive antisubmarine warfare capability and Reagan's call for ballistic missile defense, would have to look to a cautious Russian war planner like a first-strike capability.[61] In concrete terms, could the USSR feel secure in the face of U.S. deployment of the MX, B-1, cruise missiles, and the Trident II?

Given current technology and each side's beliefs, it may be that only one side can have a fairly high degree of security. There is nothing necessarily faulty about a doctrine which says that that side should be the West. This seems to be the position taken in Weinberger's first Defense Guidance (a classified Pentagon planning document), which apparently says that "United States nuclear capabilities must prevail even under the condition of prolonged war."[62] But it is contradictory to couple this posture with claims that mutual security is sought and that the adversary should not feel threatened by American requirements and deployments.[63] To put this another way, although many of the expositions of the countervailing strategy say that the problem it is designed to meet is Soviet nuclear superiority, a return to parity would not meet the strategy's goals. Parity would not allow the United States to launch a first nuclear strike in response to a Soviet attack on Europe or provide options which could be implemented at reasonably low risk. The requirement that the United States deny the Soviets any military advantage from a move might be met with forces equal to those of the Soviets in a world in which technology and geography gave the defense the advantage (that is, one in which it took larger forces to attack than to defend),[64] but given Western weaknesses in conventional arms, superiority in some higher levels of violence would probably be needed.

Does American Foreign Policy Require the Countervailing Strategy?

The last major contradiction in countervailing power may not seem central, but it is linked to important general issues of how threats exert influence. The same people who deny that American strategic forces are sufficient for its foreign policy often claim that the United States should (and therefore presumably can) follow a more assertive foreign policy. Thus Henry Kissinger has argued that the current strategic balance is intolerable, but also has called for a firmer U.S. response to Soviet adventures in Africa. But if the supposed weakness in U.S. foreign policy is the product of faulty judgment rather than insufficient strategic power, why are more weapons and a new doctrine needed? On this point, as on many others, Paul Nitze is consistent: he argued that unless and until the United States has built up its strategic forces, it has to conduct its foreign policy from a position of weakness. But Harold Brown, while calling for new military programs, insists that "it is simply a myth that . . . the United States has suffered a major loss of leverage because of the Soviet nuclear buildup. It is equally untrue that the supposed loss of U.S. nuclear superiority makes us any less willing to act than in those days when the Soviets threatened our allies in Europe over Suez, made life exceedingly difficult over Berlin, or deployed missiles to Cuba."[65]

The contradiction is epitomized by Brown's statements about the Soviet threat to American interests in the Persian Gulf. Although members of the Carter administration had said that nuclear deterrence was no longer credible enough to protect widespread American interests in areas like this, when a threat to the Gulf was discovered, the United States promised to use nuclear weapons if need be. Secretary Brown argued, consistent with the theme of this book but not with the assumptions and arguments of the countervailing strategy, that because "the Soviets couldn't count on" any conflict in the Gulf remaining limited to that region, "we don't have to match them battalion for battalion on the ground." Regardless of the local balance, invasion of the Gulf is "not a safe option" because it could lead to "global nuclear war." Similarly, Reagan said that the U.S. does not need "the stationing of enough troops [so] that . . . we could stop the Soviet Union if they set out to advance." Rather what is called for is "a presence [so] that we're there enough . . . for the Soviets to know that if they made a reckless move, they would be risking a confrontation with the United States." When asked why this was not "an empty threat that the Soviets could see through," he replied: "it's based on the assumption—and I think a correct assumption—[that] the Soviet Union is not ready to take on that confrontation which could become World War III."[66]

[5]

Escalation Dominance and Competition in Risk-Taking

IS DETERRENCE WITHOUT DEFENSE POSSIBLE?

The final contradiction presented in the last chapter raises a central issue that we have circled around throughout this book: Can a country have the means of deterrence without that of defense? For example, in order to deter a Soviet attack in the Persian Gulf, must the West be physically able to block Russian conquest of the area, as many pronouncements on the countervailing strategy imply? Or, is the position taken by Brown and Reagan in the statements just quoted acceptable—can the United States deter an attack even though its defense capabilities are inadequate? Can the threat to use force be credible when the force will not directly prevent the other side from reaching its goal? Many proponents of the countervailing strategy suggest that it cannot. This position was most clearly put by General Russell Dougherty, a former commander-in-chief of SAC, when he argued that "we operate on the principle that our deterrent contribution will be a direct reflection of our ability to fight effectively—no matter what a potential aggressor might do."[1] Colin Gray's view is similar: "If Soviet military power cannot be denied its military goals . . . none of the other possible U.S. war-waging schemes (countereconomic and political control targeting, for leading examples) are likely to have an intolerable and enduring effect. In short, to misquote General Douglas MacArthur, 'there is no substitute for victory-denial.' "[2]

Official doctrine is more ambiguous on this point. The issue is, of course, related to the question discussed earlier of the need to deny the Soviets any gains from aggression, so two statements by Secretary Brown will serve here to reveal the position and its problems: "we must ensure that no adversary would see himself better off after a limited exchange than before it. We cannot permit an enemy to believe that he could create any kind of military or psychological asymmetry that he could then exploit to his advantage." "Our countervailing strategy seeks to deny the Soviets victory, and an improved relative balance would appear to be a minimum condition of 'victory.' "[3]

The essential point in considering the meaning and validity of these statements is the simplest one: barring an unforeseen technological breakthrough which would repeal the nuclear revolution, neither side will be able to gain a "victory" or even a "military advantage" in the sense of being able to guarantee the protection of its society during a war. If there is a war and cities and other values are spared, the reason will be that the adversary was persuaded to do so, not that he was deprived of the ability to destroy them. The implications of this vulnerability point in two opposing directions. First, if no outcome which leaves a state decimated can be considered a victory, then it is easy to have the ability to deny victory to the other side. (We will return to the crucial question of what makes a threat to carry out such destruction credible.) Second, if deterrence without defense is a chimera and what is needed is the ability not only to destroy the other, but also to protect oneself, then the goal is beyond either superpower's reach.

If one tries to argue for a middle position—that denying the Russians any military advantage contributes strongly to deterrence and may even be necessary for it—problems abound. Taken literally, Brown's statement means that the United States needs the ability to ensure that the Russians could not believe that a limited nuclear exchange would leave them better off according to some measure of nuclear power than they were before the war—for instance, a better ratio vis-à-vis remaining Western warheads, megatonnage, or hard-target kill ability. To simplify, let us look only at warheads. Brown's position implies that the United States needs something that is impossible in an era of accurate MIRVs and fixed land-based forces. Under these conditions, attacking the other's ICBMs will yield a warhead ratio vis-à-vis the other which is better than the one that existed before the strike. But it is hard to see this as terribly disturbing. As I noted earlier, no one is much concerned over the long-standing vulnerability of submarines in port, which would allow the Soviets to destroy hundreds of American warheads with only a few of their own. Furthermore, Brown and others who share his views have endorsed the deployment of the heavily MIRVed MX in silos, a move that will make it even harder for the United States to meet Brown's requirement.

It can be argued that these situations are not dangerous because although the Russians could improve their military position, they could not gain a meaningful advantage over the United States. In other words, what is important is not ensuring that the Russians would not be better off after the strike than before it, but seeing that their post-strike position was not sufficient to permit them to exact concessions. This makes a bit more sense, but still is not entirely clear since it raises in slightly different form the question of what superiority means. Does it mean that the Russians would be able to outlast the United States in a counterforce war of attrition? That the Soviets could destroy enough American warheads so that the United States could not attack large numbers of OMT and leadership targets? (In the latter case, it should be noted, the relevant comparison is not between American and Soviet warheads but between American warheads and Soviet targets.) In either case, military advantage would be useful only if it could be translated into an ability to terminate the war on acceptable terms. These terms would have to include keeping one's society intact, which could be accomplished only by mutual restraint. Why should the Russians believe that the probability of maintaining this restraint would be greater if they were able to gain an advantage in warheads than it would if they were not?

This analysis casts a somewhat different light on the familiar problem of crisis instability, the condition that exists when a state would rather launch a first strike than receive one. Usually this is taken to mean that a first strike would be militarily advantageous because the side striking first would reduce the other's capability more than it reduces its own. But to focus on the gain or loss of military power is to distort the pressures both states will feel. Looking at the problem from the broader context of the existence of mutual vulnerability shows that the situation is at once more dangerous and less dangerous than the standard approach implies. On the one hand, as long as war is not believed to be inevitable, a degree of crisis instability may not be particularly troublesome because the military advantage which could be gained from a first strike offers no real protection.[4] On the other hand, even when shooting first uses up more capability than it destroys on the other side, a state might want to do so in the belief that moving first with a limited strike would demonstrate its resolve and convince the other side to back down. Just as the United States wanted to move first in the Cuban missile crisis by establishing a blockade before the Russians could commit themselves to standing firm, so in a much more desperate situation a state could view bargaining advantages as outweighing the military costs of moving first.

ESCALATION DOMINANCE VERSUS
COMPETITION IN RISK-TAKING

The attempt to escape the nuclear revolution by acquiring the capacity for deterrence by denial is misguided. This capability is not necessary to deter the Soviet Union from adventures and would not produce the desired degree of security even if it were achieved. The enormous costs of a nuclear war—and the costs and risks of lower levels of violence—mean that fear and tolerance of punishment are crucial in modern wars and confrontations. To explore this issue more fully and examine the central issue of the dynamics of bargaining and credibility, we should focus on two conflicting views of the role of force: escalation dominance and "competition in risk-taking."[5] By the latter I mean, following Thomas Schelling, that when all-out war will destroy both sides, maneuvering short of that level of violence is very strongly influenced by each side's willingness to run risks. As I will discuss below, this willingness is not closely linked to the military balance, since military advantage cannot protect the state from destruction. Escalation dominance, by contrast, means having military capabilities that can contain or defeat the adversary at all levels of violence with the possible exception of the highest. (The last phrase is needed because it is hard to talk of one side's having an advantage in an unrestrained nuclear war.) Thus Weinberger argues that deterrence of nuclear war requires that "the Soviets recognize that our forces can and will deny them their objectives at whatever level of nuclear conflict they contemplate."[6] Those who stress the importance of this capacity argue that in the hands of an aggressor it is a strong tool for expansion, and in the hands of a defender it greatly eases the task of maintaining the status quo. If the Russians possessed escalation dominance in Europe, they could launch a war in relative safety because no matter what the West did, it would lose. If NATO did not escalate, it would be defeated. Tactical nuclear weapons would not alter the outcome; they would only create more casualties on both sides. Escalation to limited strategic nuclear war would likewise fail because of superior Russian capability on this level also. The West would be in a very weak position, not only having to bear the onus of escalating at each stage, but unable to prevent a Soviet conquest of Europe by doing so. Thus Senator Sam Nunn's conclusion: "Under conditions of strategic parity and theater nuclear inferiority, a NATO nuclear response to non-nuclear Soviet aggression in Europe would be a questionable strategy at best, a self-defeating one at worst."[7]

Equally, if the West were in a position of escalation dominance the Soviets would be stymied. They would not be able to conquer Western Europe at any level of violence, assuming (and, as we will see, this apparently straightforward assumption is problematic) that the West matched the Soviet behavior—that is, used conventional forces against their conventional army, employed tactical nuclear weapons if they did, and responded to their initiation of limited strategic nuclear strikes with similar moves. Nitze has made a similar argument on the strategic level: "If our counterforce capabilities, survivable after an initial Soviet strike, were sufficient to out-match Soviet residual forces, while our other forces were capable of holding Soviet population and industry in reciprocal danger to our own, the quality of deterrence would be high because the Soviets would know we were in a position to implement a credible military strategy in the event deterrence were to fail."[8]

These arguments rest on three beliefs: that what matters most is what is happening on the battlefield; that deterrence without defense is difficult if not impossible; and that the threat to escalate lacks credibility unless a state can defeat the other side on the level of violence it is threatening to move to (otherwise escalation will only raise costs on both sides).

In criticizing this position I will assume that both sides can predict the military impact of moving to a higher level of violence and that these predictions agree. Given the unprecedented nature of the war, the difficulty of assessing the balance, and the differences between the two sides' perspectives, this is a gross oversimplification. In the actual event, neither NATO nor the USSR could be sure that escalation would not reverse their military fortunes. But the simplification is useful because the situation it assumes is the hardest case for my argument to deal with.

The first problem with the logic of escalation dominance is

[131]

that a state confident of winning at a given level of violence may yet be deterred because it judges the cost of fighting at that level to be excessive. The other side of this coin is that even if defense cannot succeed, the threat to defend can deter if the potential attacker thinks that the status-quo power is sufficiently strongly motivated to be willing to fight for what it knows will be a losing cause. Nuclear weapons have not changed the fact that victory is not worthwhile if the costs entailed are greater than the gains. Thus Michael Howard calls for a buildup of NATO's conventional forces even if they could not prevent a Soviet victory on the grounds that "the Soviet leadership has to be brought to see that, even if there were no escalation to nuclear war, their armed forces would suffer so severely at the hands of the defenders of Western Europe that the cost of any military achievements would be unacceptably high in terms, not only of blood and treasure, but of the cohesion of their Empire."[9]

Escalation in a Losing Cause

But what credibility is there in the threat to fight what would be a losing battle? Often, quite a bit: such behavior is common—states usually resist conquest. Even if a state knows it will lose if an adversary persists, the reasons for fighting are several. National honor is one. The desire to harm and weaken the enemy is another, often coupled with the hope of earning a place at the conference table if their allies eventually win. Finally, and most important here, if the state can raise the cost of conquest higher than the value the other side will gain in victory, it can make the contest into a game of Chicken. That is, although war will lead to the state's defeat, the adversary will prefer to make concessions rather than fight. So even when it is obvious that war would damage the state more than the adversary, this does not mean the latter can be sure that the former will not fight; the game of Chicken does not have a determinative solution. Furthermore, if the war lasts a considerable length of time, the adversary may reach the breaking point before the defender,

[132]

realizing that even though it can win, the price will be excessive. The United States withdrew from Vietnam even though no one doubted that victory was possible.

Increasing the Costs to the Other Side

The second and third lines of rebuttal to the escalation-dominance position stress that the focus on the battlefield, which is a form of conventionalization, is misleading. The second counterargument is that in order to raise the cost to its opponent, the side that is losing can move to a higher level of violence even if it does not believe it can win at that level. A state which realizes this can be deterred even if it thinks it can win the war. For example, when Italy invaded Ethiopia, Britain refrained from attacking the Italian navy not because the British could not have prevailed, but because the expected damage to their own navy was seen to outweigh the benefits. Thus it is not correct to claim that a threat to escalate will be credible if and only if it is believed the action will bring a military victory; one must consider the price that both sides would have to pay. To use a version of Michael Howard's example, the United States might deter a Soviet invasion of Western Europe by threatening to use tactical nuclear weapons even if the Russians believed that they could win such a war. To gain control of Europe at the cost of having much of Eastern Europe and the Red Army destroyed might not be a good bargain.

But why would a state be willing to escalate if doing so would not bring victory? In the case of the American use of tactical nuclear weapons, such escalation would make a great deal of sense if the American decision-makers believed that war could be kept to this level of violence. For in that case the Soviet Union (and the Europeans) would pay most of the price; although the U.S. army in Europe would presumably be destroyed, the American homeland would remain untouched. Even without this added incentive, however, escalation could be a rational choice for the same reasons that fighting in a losing

[133]

cause would be: national honor, the desire to harm and weaken those who represent abhorred values, and the belief that the other will retreat rather than pay the price which can be exacted for victory.

The third and most important reason why it is incorrect to concentrate on who can win on the battlefield is that the war may spread even if no one wants it to. The use of force involves a significant but hard-to-measure possibility of mutually un-desired escalation. A state unable to win on the battlefield could thus rationally enter into a conflict in the belief that the other side would rather concede than engage in a struggle which could escalate. Similarly, a state with escalation dominance might avoid a confrontation in the knowledge that while it would win a limited war, the risk that the conflict would ex-pand was excessive. The common claim that militarily effective options are needed is not correct. A state can increase the cost to the other side by making limited attacks on the other's soci-ety or by taking other actions that increase the chance of un-desired escalation.

A state unwilling to wage all-out war in responding to a major provocation could rationally decide to take actions which it believed entailed, say, a 10 percent chance of leading to such a war. (The difficulty of making such an estimate does not effect the basic point.) The threat to do so could be "implementable," to use Schlesinger's term, and the result can be deterrence with-out the ability to deny the other its objectives. For example, the Russians would be deterred from invading Western Europe even if they enjoyed escalation dominance if they believed that probable Western responses would create an unacceptable risk of world war. Risk, of course, puts pressures on both sides. But a given level of risk may be acceptable to the defender of the status quo and intolerable to an aggressor; the threat to raise the risk to a given level may be credible when made by the former and not credible when made by the latter. The fact that deter-rence is usually easier than compellence aids the status-quo power.[10]

Risk-Taking and Military Advantage

What is crucial in this context is that the ability to tolerate and raise the level of risk is not closely tied to military superiority. Because the credibility of the threat to escalate is not determined by the military effectiveness of the action, escalation dominance does not give any state a great advantage. If NATO leaders were willing to tolerate increased destruction and increased risk of all-out war, they could escalate from conventional to tactical nuclear warfare even if they did not expect this action to turn the tide of battle. On the other hand, if they believed escalation could halt the Russian invasion, but only at an intolerable risk of all-out war, their position would be weak. (The perceived risk of escalation depends in part on one's estimate of the risks the other side is willing to run. If NATO leaders thought the USSR would back down quickly in the face of NATO's use of tactical nuclear weapons, they would see using them as less risky. If the Soviets were seen as willing to tolerate a high level of danger, by contrast, then escalation would appear more dangerous, since the USSR would be believed ready to maintain or increase the level of violence, with the attendant risk that the war could spread further. In other words, the familiar interactive dynamics of the Chicken game come into play.)

The links between military power—both local and global—and states' behavior in crisis are thus tenuous. Escalation dominance does not make it safe to stand firm. As Thomas Schelling points out, "Being able to lose a local war in a dangerous and provocative manner may make the risk . . . outweigh the apparent gains to the other side." Similarly, even "if the tactical advantages are unimpressive, one's purpose in enlarging some limited war may be to confront the enemy with a heightened risk."[11] The exact location of the battle lines and the question whether American troops are pushing back Soviet forces or vice versa matter much less than each side's beliefs about whether the war can be kept limited. This is true not only for warfare in

Europe or the Persian Gulf, but also for nuclear counterforce wars. Imagine a situation in which the Russians believed that they could gain advantages, in terms of various measures of residual strategic forces, over the United States in a missile duel. What would they gain thereby? As Warner Schilling has noted, "the strategic debate has focused on numbers of missiles and warheads as if they were living creatures whose survival was of value in their own right, to the near exclusion of any effort to relate these military means to potential differences in the war outcomes among which statesmen might actually be able to discriminate in terms of the values about which they do care."[12] Since a state cannot protect itself by destroying many of the other side's weapons, an advantage in remaining warheads could help it reach an acceptable termination of the war only if its adversary was persuaded or coerced into sparing cities.

This outcome might be the result if both sides waged a purely counterforce war, although even then the destruction would be so great that the costs to the "winner" might well outweigh the gains. But even if the Russians were confident that they would come out ahead in this contest, could they expect that the United States would limit its response to Soviet strategic forces and exhaust its forces while leaving Soviet cities intact? The reply, of course, is that the United States would be restrained by the Soviet threat to respond in kind. But the crucial point is that each side's hold over the other's cities is not affected by who is "ahead" in the counterforce exchange. It is hard to imagine the Russians thinking "that in the aftermath of a Soviet nuclear strike . . . an American president [would] tote up the residual megatonnage or [warheads] of both sides and sue for peace or even surrender if his side came up short."[13]

Now that the state which is losing can do overwhelming damage to the superior power, military superiority even on several levels is not controlling. In discussing the Cuban missile crisis, Bernard Brodie puts the point very well. "The essential question was: How much did the strictly local forces affect the Russians' willingness to open hostilities with us—or, for that matter, our willingness to get into such hostilities with them? And the answer clearly was, little or none—unless both sides had been completely convinced that a quite considerable shooting war could develop on the spot without its substantially widening and incurring extremely grave risk of nuclear weapons being introduced."[14] In the late 1960s, a reporter asked an Air Force general whether the United States could "effectively support Israel in the event of a joint Soviet-Egyptian attack." The general replied: "Forget it. With the Soviet Air Force in Egypt and the Soviet naval squadron in the Mediterranean, we couldn't get close." The fallacy in this argument is again noted by Brodie: "With respect to the chances of getting into a conflict with the other superpower, the Soviet Union, like the United States, is always looking past local forces."[15]

Resolve and Threats That Leave Something to Chance

The threat of escalation implicit in the limited use of force acts through two related mechanisms, neither of which is linked to the local military balance. First, the use of force demonstrates a state's resolve, its willingness to run high risks rather than retreat. It provides evidence that the state will continue to fight and even escalate further unless a satisfactory settlement can be arranged. Of course it does not prove this; the state may be bluffing or its resolve may melt in the face of a firm response. But it gives some credibility to its threats. For example, during the Cuban missile crisis it seems that Kennedy's "quest for a means of impressing Khrushchev with his determination was provided . . . by United States naval harassment of . . . Soviet submarines."[16]

The second mechanism involves the threat of unintended as opposed to intended escalation. As Brodie points out, "violence between great opponents is inherently difficult to control."[17] The implications are best discussed by Thomas Schelling, whose formulation I cannot improve upon:

The idea . . . that a country cannot plausibly threaten to engage in

[137]

a general war over anything but a mortal assault on itself unless it has an appreciable capacity to blunt the other side's attack seems to depend on the clean-cut notion that war results—or is expected to result—only from a deliberate yes-no decision. But if war tends to result from a process, a dynamic process in which both sides get more and more concerned not to be a slow second in case the war starts, it is not a "credible first strike" that one threatens, but just plain war. The Soviet Union can indeed threaten us with war: they can even threaten us with a war that we eventually start, by threatening to get involved with us in a process that blows up into war. And some of the arguments about "superiority" and "inferiority" seem to imply that one of the two sides, being weaker, must absolutely fear and concede while the other, being stronger, may confidently expect the other to yield. There is undoubtedly a good deal to the notion that the country with the less impressive military capability may be less feared, and the other may run the riskier course in a crisis; other things being equal, one anticipates that the strategically "superior" country has some advantage. But this is a far cry from the notion that the two sides just measure up to each other and one bows before the other's superiority and acknowledges that he was only bluffing. Any situation that scares one side will scare both sides with the danger of a war that neither wants, and both will have to pick their way carefully through the crisis, never quite sure that the other knows how to avoid stumbling over the brink.[18]

Schelling's concept of the threat that leaves something to chance is crucial to understanding this process.[19] This is the threat to do something which could lead to still further escalation even though the state might not want that to occur. Any time military forces are set in motion, there is a danger that things will get out of control. Statesmen cannot be sure that they will; if they could be, then the threat to take initial action would be no more credible than the threat to wage all-out war. But no one can be sure that they will not; the workings of machines and the reaction of humans in time of stress cannot be predicted with high confidence. Morton Halperin has pointed out that there are two kinds of escalation: one that results from an explicit decision to increase the scope, area, or level of violence in a measured fashion and the other that involves an unintended "explosion" and a disastrous leap to all-out war.[20] Willingness to engage in the former implies a belief that the latter is not inevitable, but it also exerts pressures by increasing the chance that the latter will occur.

Because confrontations and the use of violence unleash forces whose results cannot be predicted with confidence, states can deter a wide range of transgressions without making specific threats about what they will do in the event that the other takes the forbidden actions. The deterrent may be effective even if the threat to respond, when viewed as an isolated act, is not. This point is missed by those who hold the frequently expressed view that the American "threat of nuclear response has . . . lost credibility with respect to Western Europe and has virtually none at all as a deterrent to Soviet action in China, Southwest Asia, or Eastern Europe."[21] This claim is probably valid for the contingency that the United States would use nuclear weapons as an immediate response to a Soviet invasion of China or Iran. But the common phrase "the credibility of the American threat" is misleading. The problem the Soviets face is not only that the United States might fulfill any commitments it had made, but also that their action could start a process the end result of which would be disaster. Could the Russians really be confident that a major attack on China would not lead to the involvement of U.S. strategic forces, especially if Chinese and Soviet nuclear weapons were employed? Could they be certain that the use of military force in the Persian Gulf would not lead to a general war?

It is in the wider context of the possible chain of effects which violent change in the status quo could set off that the influence of nuclear weapons must be seen. A state may then be deterred even if it is sure that its adversary's initial response will not be to carry out its threat; states contemplating expansion must be concerned not with how their efforts would begin, but how they would end. If the Russians attacked Europe and NATO resisted, nuclear war could readily result even if the United

States did not immediately launch SAC. States cannot carefully calibrate the level of risks that they are running. They cannot be sure how close they are to the brink of war. (Indeed during the Cuban missile crisis Robert Kennedy suggested that enforcing the blockade might be too dangerous and that "it was better to knock out the missiles by air attack than to stop a Soviet ship on the high seas."[22])

Although undesired escalation obviously does not occur all the time,[23] the danger is always present. The room for misunderstanding, the pressure to act before the other side has seized the initiative, the role of unexpected defeats or unanticipated opportunities, all are sufficiently great—and interacting—so that it is rare that decision-makers can confidently predict the end-point of the trajectory which an initial resort to violence starts.

Statesmen understand this uncertainty and use it. As one British diplomat recorded during the Munich crisis, the foreign secretary "would like to say to Ribbentrop that no one in Great Britain wants to fight for Czechoslovakia but if Czechoslovakia were attacked, there would be very great risk of a general conflagration in which we should be inevitably dragged in." Similar words were used by the British foreign secretary on the eve of World War I, when he told his ambassador to Berlin: "if war does take place we may be drawn into it by the development of other issues."[24] As I noted at the end of the last chapter, Brown and Reagan rested American deterrence policy in the Persian Gulf on this mechanism. Caspar Weinberger makes the same point when he stresses the "clear Soviet understanding of the certainty that a conventional/nuclear war in Europe risks engagement of the central nuclear systems of the United States."[25]

Willingness to Run Risks

Of course in the Czech crisis it was Britain, rather than Germany, which backed down. Because the threat that leaves something to chance exerts pressure on both sides, it is not an automatic way to protect the status quo. The function of crises, then, is to create risks which, given the existence of mutual vulnerability, will bring pressure to bear on both sides. As Brodie argued soon after the Cuban missile conflict, the fact that states can take actions which create "'some' risk [of nuclear war] is what makes [crisis bargaining] possible. We rarely have to threaten general war. We threaten instead the next in a series of moves that seems to tend in that direction. The opponent has the choice of making the situation more dangerous, or less so. This is all pretty obvious when stated, but so much of the theorizing . . . about the inapplicability of the nuclear deterrent to the future overlooks this simple fact."[26]

Indeed it is missed by those who stress the importance of escalation dominance. If confrontations and crises can get out of hand and lead to total war, advantages on the battlefield have little significance. They are hard to translate into successful war termination and as long as conflict continues, both sides will be primarily concerned with the danger of all-out war. Thus crises and limited wars involving both superpowers are competitions in risk-taking. A state which has gained battlefield victories but finds the risks implicit in continued fighting intolerable will be likely to make concessions; a state which is losing on the ground but finds this verdict so painful that it is willing to undergo still higher levels of pain and danger is likely to prevail.[27] What is often crucial, then, are each side's judgments of the chances that the conflict will expand, the willingness of each to bear costs and risks, and its perceptions of the other's willingness to do so.

These truths will be lost and we will be misled if we focus on military solutions. Eugene Rostow, when director of the Arms Control and Disarmament Agency, said that the United States needs forces such that "we can control situations where our interests are affected and where diplomacy does fail through the use of conventional forces without fear that escalation will take place to a level where we no longer can function."[28] But even magnificent forces cannot give the United States this "control," and so military advantage cannot allow it to fight "without fear that escalation will take place."

Although Fred Iklé is a proponent of the countervailing strategy, he understands this danger when he argues: "The more firmly NATO leaders expected that a conventional war in Europe would develop into a nuclear war, the more anxious they would be to terminate the fighting if a conventional war actually broke out. Every day, every hour, the conventional campaigns were being fought would seem to prolong that risk of imminent nuclear war."[29] This line of argument is implicit in the many American statements which express doubt as to whether a Soviet-American clash could be kept limited, for example: "there are severe risks that any U.S.–Soviet—or any NATO/Warsaw Pact—confrontation that led to the use of military forces would end in [maximum] destruction, whatever the pre-crisis intentions of the parties."[30] What is crucial is that the pressures to which Iklé points apply irrespective of the military balance.

This analysis refutes the basic position of the countervailing strategy put forth by Harold Brown which shares Rostow's incorrect starting point—the importance of maintaining military advantage: the United States "seek(s) to convince the Soviets that they could not win . . . a [limited] war, and thus to deter them from starting one."[31] While this ability probably contributes to deterrence, it is not necessary for it. Being able to do better than the adversary in a limited war does not make it safe to engage in such a conflict. For example, it was fear of unpredictable escalation rather than lack of military options which led the Truman administration to refrain from expanding the Korean conflict to encompass the enemy forces in China. Likewise, the Soviet Union has long been deterred from moving against Berlin not by lack of local superiority, but by fear of escalation, either intended or uncontrolled. (As Brodie noted, the argument that the Soviets retreated during the Cuban missile crisis because of their military weakness in the area is undercut by their simultaneous passivity in Berlin where they had the military advantage.[32]) It is important to remember that the costs of a conflict include not only the losses incurred at that level of violence, but also the danger of undesired consequences which are not under the complete control of either party. Luckily, decision-makers are less apt to overlook this than are analysts. Thus Glenn Synder and Paul Diesing found that in thirteen out of sixteen cases of crisis bargaining they studied, "decision-makers felt fears of varying intensity that the crisis might go out of control, either because of unauthorized acts by subordinates or client states or because of spiraling anger and hostility, popular or governmental," Indeed, the statesmen seem to have exaggerated the dangers in these cases.[33]

Thus it is clear that escalation dominance is not necessary for deterrence. In principle it is not sufficient for deterrence either. A state superior at all levels of violence could decide to allow its adversary to alter the status quo rather than pay the price of a limited conflict and the chance of escalation to mutually unacceptable levels. I cannot think of any important cases which fit this description, however. States do not seem able to use the lever of competition in risk-taking to force others to abandon territory they control or positions of influence they have established.[34] For example, Japan would not have attacked Pearl Harbor, Malaya, and the Philippines unless it expected local victories. Although doing so would not have been totally irrational if it believed that the costs of a major war would have been higher for Britain and the United States than those entailed in giving Japan a sphere of influence in China and Southeast Asia,[35] it is hard to imagine Japan moving if it had thought the war would have gone badly from the start.

The case of Italy, Ethiopia, and Britain in 1935–36 is also interesting in this regard. As I noted, Italy was able to deter British military intervention through the potential punishment it could inflict. In principle, this leverage might have been effective even in the absence of superiority over Ethiopia. That is, Italy might have coerced Britain into pressuring Ethiopia to make concessions by threatening a naval war with England. But this seems implausible, in part because the credibility of the threat would have been impaired by the requirement that to implement it Italy would have had to bear the onus of starting the naval war that both sides wanted to avoid. Of course, Italy could have initiated either the war with Ethiopia (which, in this hypothetical example, it knew it could not win) or some other conflict with Britain to set off a chance of undesired escalation, thereby putting intolerable pressure on the British decision-makers. But actual cases like this are hard to find.

Anwar Sadat's 1973 war with Israel provides ambiguous evidence on this point. On the one hand, the Egyptians seem to have expected to gain at least a local and short-run victory and probably would not have attacked had they believed they could make no military progress. On the other hand, the political gains they made were only tenuously linked to their initial military victory. Instead, altering the status quo became possible because all parties gained a new appreciation for the dangers of trying to maintain the 1967 boundary lines. Had Egypt started losing at the beginning (which might have brought about an even greater degree of superpower involvement), the result might have been the same.[36]

So it can be argued that although the United States does not need escalation dominance, it would be added insurance. Possibly, but the historical record may not be an adequate guide to the future. Beyond that, we should note the financial costs involved, the probable decrease in the chances for arms-control and political understandings with the Soviet Union, and the dangers which would accompany a Russian belief that the United States was seeking a first-strike capability.

Soviet Views

Although the Soviets ridicule the notion of using nuclear weapons for political bargaining, they understand the dangers and uses of unintended escalation very well. As Benjamin Lambeth has shown, their writings are full of appreciation for the unpredictability of military ventures.[37] The same attitude was revealed by Khrushchev during the Cuban missile crisis. In his

letter to Kennedy which opened the way for an agreement, he
said:

> If you have not lost command of yourself and realize clearly what
> this could lead to, then, Mr. President, you and I should not now
> pull on the ends of the rope in which you have tied a knot of war,
> because the harder you and I pull, the tighter this knot will be-
> come. And a time may come when this knot is tied so tight that
> the person who tied it is no longer capable of untying it, and then
> the knot will have to be cut. What that would mean I need not
> explain to you, because you yourself understand perfectly what
> dread forces our two countries possess.[38]

Khrushchev also clearly perceived the role of the limited use of
force in this process for he stressed the need "to avert contact of
our ships, and, consequently, a deepening of the crisis, which
because of this contact can spark off the fire of military conflict,
after which any talks would be superfluous because other forces
and other laws would begin to operate—the laws of war." After
the crisis, he justified his concessions in terms of the prudence
required by "the smell of scorching in the air."[39] So whatever
doctrinal differences exist between the United States and the
USSR, they do not seem to affect this point. It is possible, of
course, that if American leaders argue loudly and persuasively
enough that nuclear war can be controlled, the Soviets will lose
their fear. This could be particularly dangerous because there is
some evidence that the Soviets are willing to engage in provocations when they think they can control the risks and pull back to
safety if their probes create a dangerous situation.[40] But at this
point the Russians show a healthy skepticism toward the idea
that control is easy or even possible.

As long as decision-makers realize that things can get out of
hand, crises and the limited use of force will have most of their
impact because they generate risks even if neither side explicitly
affirms this view. In other words, I am not arguing that the
United States is facing a choice between escalation dominance

[145]

and competition in risk-taking as ways of bringing pressure to bear. Even though it can choose the former as the basis for declaratory and procurement policy, it cannot escape from the fact that in tense situations, decision-makers are going to be preoccupied with the danger of all-out war. Since military advantage cannot control the risk of escalation, the attempt to banish this element cannot succeed no matter what Western policy is.

Similarly, mutual assured destruction exists as a fact, irrespective of policy. No amount of flexibility, no degree of military superiority at levels less than all-out war, can change the fundamental attribute of the nuclear age. Not only can each side destroy the other if it chooses, but that outcome can grow out of conflict even if no one wants it to. Most of the dilemmas of U.S. defense policy stem from the vulnerability of its cities, not from policies which might permit the Soviets marginal military advantages in unlikely and terribly risky contingencies. Once each side can destroy the other, any crisis brings up the possibility of this disastrous outcome. Standing firm, although often necessary, has a significant degree of risk which cannot be much reduced by the development of a wider range of military options. Carrying out actions that are militarily effective does not take one's society out of hostage; what undercuts the credibility of the American threats is not that they cannot deny the Soviets any gain or advantage, but that carrying them out may lead to disaster.

[6]

Conclusions

Unfortunately, it is easier to be critical than constructive, easier to see the flaws in established doctrine than to develop a good alternative. This is especially true on this subject because no nuclear policy can be very good. But a critical evaluation of current doctrine may not be a bad way to begin understanding what is needed. The countervailing strategy is led into many inconsistencies, incoherences, and contradictions because it seeks to repeal the nuclear revolution rather than coming to grips with the inevitable vulnerability of American society or utilizing the inevitable Soviet vulnerability. Seeking a return to the familiar world in which military advantage could be more readily translated into political achievements, American thinking too often falls into the trap of conventionalization. Trying to give nuclear weapons a firm military basis by stressing the ability to thwart the adversary at any level of violence leads to an excessive stress on the military results of less than all-out wars. The pressures fear of escalation exerts on both sides are glossed over, with the result that the credibility of the threats that the United States can now implement is underestimated and the increase in credibility which the projected capabilities would bring is exaggerated.

These points are clearly brought out by Harold Brown when he argued that "if we try [nuclear] bluffing, ways can be found by others to test our bluffs without undue risk to them."[1] Twin defects mar this position. First, as I have stressed, dangerous situations can lead to escalation even if both sides desire to keep them under control. The poker game model of bluffing is misleading. The Russians have to ask themselves what the results of an adventure might be, not what American intentions are. Second, while perhaps the risks of such probes can be limited, they can never be eliminated—especially not in the case of a move which would drastically alter the status quo, such as an attack on Europe. Nor are the risks of such a move closely linked to the military balance.

THE STABILITY-INSTABILITY PARADOX AND TWO MEANINGS OF THREAT

Many of the defects of the countervailing strategy stem from an excessive stress on the stability-instability paradox. The felt need to be able to deny the Russians an advantage at any level of violence comes in part from seeing each level as separate, from failing to appreciate the multiple ways escalation can occur, and thus downgrading the importance of the chance that a conflict will intensify. In a world with perfect control and none of Clausewitz's friction, the stability of the strategic nuclear balance would permit quite a bit of freedom for adventures at lower levels. But in the real world the effect of that stability, although not trivial, is not so powerful. Neither superpower can confidently move into an area of significant concern to the other without great risk of incurring very high costs—if not immediately, then as the result of a chain of actions that cannot be entirely foreseen or controlled.

In many cases the levels of violence, which seem separate in the abstract, blend into one another because of the way forces are arranged. Thus Brodie's telling argument as to why conventional defense of Europe is not necessary: for the Russians to attack in the face of NATO's tactical nuclear weapons would be to put their army at risk.[2] Even if Soviet and American leaders both believed that the Warsaw Pact countries could win a tacti-

[148]

cal nuclear war, could the former be confident that this would deter Western use of tactical weapons? Furthermore, as Barry Posen has shown, a conventional war on at least part of the NATO front would lead to attacks against targets which would involve Soviet nuclear forces.[3] Similarly, many communications systems are planned for use in both conventional and nuclear conflicts. To try to win the former kind of war would have at least some effect on one's ability to fight the latter.

Indeed, the call for the countervailing strategy and the argument for conventional defense in Europe share much of the same intellectual justification—both spring from the stability-instability paradox. Thus McNamara argues, "With huge survivable arsenals on both sides, strategic nuclear weapons have lost whatever military utility may once have been attributed to them. Their sole purpose, at present, is to deter the other side's first use of its strategic forces."[4] The logic underpinning this position is that levels of violence are sealed off from one another, which is also the central assumption of the countervailing strategy. But though the two agree that the threat of all-out nuclear war can deter only an all-out attack, they part company on the issue of the need for a range of limited nuclear options to deter the other side on those levels. The advocates of conventional defense for NATO see the move to nuclear weapons as a leap across a critical "fire break," in two linked senses. Neither side, they believe, can easily threaten to cross it, and once it is crossed the war could not be kept limited. The second characteristic leads to the first. Because the use of nuclear weapons, either strategic or tactical, would be likely to trigger an all-out war, NATO cannot credibly threaten any sort of a nuclear reply to a Soviet conventional invasion. This rejection of the possibility of limited nuclear war also leads to the rejection of those aspects of the countervailing strategy which see the need to be prepared to fight such wars. But in stressing that the impossibility of nuclear war leaves the Soviets relatively free to engage in aggression below that threshold of violence, the proponents of conventional defense build on the same intellectual foundation as does the current policy. Thus they exaggerate the freedom created by the stability of the strategic nuclear balance, neglect the role of threats that leave something to chance, and so underestimate the potency of NATO's nuclear deterrent.

Both those who see a need for a conventional defense of Europe and those who favor the countervailing strategy overlook the fact that the term "threat of mutual destruction" can be understood in two ways. One is an explicit threat on the order of "if you take certain prohibited actions, I will start an all-out nuclear war." This is not highly credible, and if it were the only kind operating, the stability-instability paradox would be crucial. But there is another sense of threat here: not an explicit promise to inflict pain, but a general danger. Any tense situation, or, even more, any forcible change in the status quo, creates a threat of mutual destruction in this sense. It is the perception of this danger which can restrain an aggressor even when he thinks a limited military adventure would be to his advantage. The fact of mutual assured destruction, then, provides security irrespective of each side's declared policies.

What and How Can the Threat of Nuclear War Deter?

But what kinds of moves can nuclear weapons deter? It seems generally agreed that the nuclear umbrella does not reach much beyond the American homeland and perhaps Western Europe. As Brown put it in 1979, "We now recognize that the strategic nuclear forces can deter only a relatively narrow range of contingencies, much smaller in range than was foreseen only 20 or 30 years ago."[5] It is a commonplace that American strategic nuclear forces cannot deter subversion, Soviet assistance to revolutionary movements, or even the use of force in areas of little importance to the West: for example, Soviet and Cuban adventures in Africa and even the Russian invasion of Afghanistan. While many of the proponents of the countervailing strategy have attributed these events to a Soviet perception of general American weakness and indecisiveness, they have not argued that a bolstered American arsenal—either nuclear or conventional—could have prevented them.

The fact that the proponents of the current strategy do not claim that their policy could have prevented these moves is interesting, for it reveals their own unspoken reservations about the strategy and the role the existence of mutual assured destruction plays even in low-level conflicts. The United States could have intervened in Angola and Ethiopia and denied the Russians local victories. It could have interdicted Soviet supply lines or sent ground troops of its own; the United States had the sorts of capabilities the countervailing doctrine calls for. They were not sufficient to deter the Soviets, and Washington did not implement the options it possessed. The obvious reason is that it was thought costs would be excessive in terms of domestic policies, in casualties that would have been incurred, and in the risk of escalation. No one thought that the Russians would launch a nuclear strike if the United States sent troops to Africa or even was so bold as to intercept and, if need be, shoot down Soviet transport planes. But what would have happened had such steps been taken was impossible to foresee, and the chance of mutually undesired costs, if not complete devastation, weighed heavily on American decision-makers.

The nuclear revolution renders coercion much more important, and brute force less important, than was true in the past. Improving its capabilities in the latter area will not permit the United States to prevail in a struggle that will be waged largely in the sphere of the former.[6] For this reason, the attempt to obviate the need for resolve by increasing military capability, despite its attractiveness, cannot succeed. The use of American armed forces to counter a Soviet military move will be risky; it is a delusion to believe that the risks can be greatly reduced or easily managed by a more favorable military balance. Indeed it is hard to think of a single undesirable international outcome which would have been reversed had the Soviet-American military balance been more favorable to the latter. Some proponents of the countervailing strategy believe that strengthening the military would bolster the confidence of the American leadership and public, damaged by the Vietnam war and, to a lesser extent, by the Iranian hostage crisis, and make possible a firmer stance toward the Soviet Union. But this plan is not likely to work, in part because the defense proposals are themselves controversial, in part because it will eventually become apparent that increased military spending has not altered the risks of confrontation. When it does, those whose confidence rested on outmoded beliefs about the connections between force and security are likely to be even less willing to act firmly than they would have been had they not previously relied on an inappropriate remedy.

Although the picture of the world I am presenting here denies that we need take seriously many of the nightmares which fuel the countervailing strategy, it is not an entirely reassuring one. The argument is that confrontations resemble the game of Chicken. If neither side is reasonable, both can be destroyed, and yet the very possibility of this dreadful outcome gives both sides a crucial common interest that can be exploited for competitive gains. When crises are generators of risk, superior military power no longer guarantees security. We could not escape from the nuclear revolution even if we were able to reestablish the kind of military balance that existed in the mid-1960s. The United States can contain Soviet challenges only by displaying a willingness to stand firm even at the risk of catastrophe. Even though occasions when doing so is necessary are likely to be very rare, the possibility of their occurring will color world politics. Both when they occur and when they are contemplated, states have strong and conflicting incentives; to moderate behavior to lower the risk of war through immediate confrontation, and to be firm in order both to avoid immediate losses and to reduce the danger that war will arise through the other side's belief that the state can always be forced to retreat.[7] Although factors such as the balance of interest and resolve influence the outcome, there is no determinative solution to the contest since each side will stand firm if it thinks the other will back down.

Conclusions

Thus the possibility always exists that either or both sides will pay an excessive price in the effort to prevail or that the result will be mutual devastation.

Why Deterrence Is Not so Difficult

But several factors make the picture less bleak. First, although resolve and perceptions of resolve are extremely important, the contest is not a zero-sum game; one side does not have to gain security entirely at the other's expense. Part of the reason for this is that resolve does not exist in a vacuum. That is, the superpowers run risks in particular contexts for particular objectives. In most situations, states are more willing to pay a high price to defend their positions than they are to try to expand. Thus the West may have, and be seen as having, high resolve to stand firm if its vital interests are challenged and the Soviets can have, and be seen as having, similarly great willingness to run risks to defend their established positions. This happy situation does not come about automatically, but its likelihood is increased by the fact that both sides know that deterrence is usually easier than compellence.[8]

A kind of symmetry reinforces this effect. Expansionist objectives which the Russians might reach at low risk are not likely to be important for either them or the West. To the extent they are not important to the latter, the United States need not be concerned. To the extent that they do not represent much gain to the Russians, the effort to attain them may not be worth even a very low risk. On the other hand, those objectives that the Russians value much more—for example, control of Western Europe—are also very important to the United States.[9] To try to seize them, therefore, would be very dangerous. Thus inhibitions against expansion tend to be highest in those cases in which it would bring significant gains. Indeed, to the extent that what is at stake in many conflicts is perceptions of how each side will behave in the future, the Russians cannot expect to make a large gain except by inflicting a large loss on the

United States—which it would not do without encountering a great deal of resistance and, therfore, taking a large risk. If the Russians thought that a victory in any dispute would be taken by all as evidence that the United States was not likely to stand firm in a range of disputes important to it, they would have to expect the United States to pay a significant price rather than retreat.

A second stabilizing factor, and an additional reason for the bargaining advantage of the side defending the existing situation, is that the expansionist must start the process of changing the status quo. In the areas of the world that matter most, furthermore, taking such action will involve using force. The aggressor must thus act in a way which will greatly increase the chance of major violence. Once it does so, the danger is a shared one. The defender must be willing to run significant risks if it is not to be forced to retreat. But the initial burden falls on the aggressor. Thus unless the Soviet Union is very highly motivated to expand (a point discussed below), the status quo will be maintained. Those who stress the problems of extended deterrence created by the stability-instability paradox point out that, lacking the ability to meet a limited military challenge on its own terms, the defender will have to bear the onus of escalation. Both sides know this, thereby weakening the defender's resolve and opening the way for the aggressor to change the status quo by threatening to use force. But to maintain this position is to overlook the fact that the aggressor is still required to take the first, and very dangerous, step. This burden would be light only if the aggressor could be sure that the defender would not escalate and that the situation would remain under control. It is hard to see how these conditions could be met.

Both the balance of resolve and the inhibitions against starting a process that could lead to World War III thus usually give the defender a political and bargaining advantage. Just as such an advantage for the defense in the military sphere eases the general problem of the security dilemma (the fact that increases in one side's security usually decrease the security of others), so the parallel advantage discussed here makes it possible for both sides to feel relatively secure in their ability to protect their established interests without simultaneously being well positioned to menace the other's values.

A third factor modifying the dangerous reliance on resolve is that in the nuclear era statesmen, in both East and West, have been more cautious than an abstract analysis of the situation facing them would lead one to expect.[10] Whereas the stability-instability paradox could lead to relentless probing in the calculation that the risks are low enough to be worth running, decision-makers have taken what Patrick Morgan calls a more "sensible" approach[11] and have generally been willing to forego the chance of gains in order to keep the risks of war as low as possible. Of course, this pattern may not continue. A bolder—or more foolish—person might come to power in Washington or Moscow, although the relative consistency of behavior over a prolonged period in which leaders with very different person-. alities have held office gives one some grounds for confidence.

Finally, the most obvious reason why the pattern is not likely to change is perhaps also the most important. The costs of a major, but still limited, nuclear war would be greater than those ever experienced; the costs of an all-out war are simply unimaginable. This creates what McGeorge Bundy has called "existential deterrence."[12] With the penalty for blundering into war so great, even bold and foolish decision-makers behave cautiously. As long as they have reason to believe that their basic position can be preserved without a war,[13] they will shy away from adventures which could lead to disaster. While sophisticated bargaining theories might indicate that statesmen can and should behave differently, the oppressive possibility of total destruction is likely to continue to lead them to be sensible. We should not forget the most basic fact of the nuclear age. The enormous costs of major war now raise more sharply the perennial question about the use of violence: What goals are worth the price?[14]

This analysis implies that all but the most highly motivated aggressors will be relatively easy to deter from attempts to use force to change important aspects of the status quo. Would the Russians launch a conventional attack in Europe or the Persian Gulf if they thought that the result would be a victory if the war stayed at that level of violence, but that there was as much as a 10 percent chance that it would not? The argument that the American threat to use nuclear weapons is not very credible glosses over the point that only a little credibility may be required. One could argue in rebuttal that deterring the Soviets calls for highly credible threats—a Hitler would not be easily restrained. I agree that the emergence of such a leader would pose incredible dangers to the whole world. But it should be remembered that the situation has changed: if Hitler's armies had succeeded, he could have protected his homeland even if his enemies had not cooperated in keeping the war limited. No Soviet Hitler could believe he could do so. Furthermore, though a very bold Soviet leader would pose a grave threat to American interests, this would be the case no matter what strategy the United States followed. If this leader believed, as Hitler did, that his adversaries would rather make major concessions than go to war, he could exert enormous pressure even if the United States had the ability to deny him any military advantage from his moves.

Although the possibility of another Hitler is not to be ignored, too much can be made of it. A lot of terrible things are possible, and the fact that Nazi Germany was a recent occurrence that is burned into our memories should not cloud our judgment as to how likely such danger is to arise again. Hitlers are very rare; the Soviet system does not seem to breed such figures (Stalin may have been as evil, but he sought to avoid, instead of welcoming, international risks). Given the kind of Soviet leaders we have seen and the risks which are automatically involved in an attack in Europe or the Persian Gulf, let alone a strike against part of the American strategic force, the difficulty of extended deterrence has been exaggerated. Of course the dangers could increase in a crisis, a point discussed below, but even in difficult circumstances, what goals would be attractive enough to the Soviets to merit risking the future of their state and world socialism? The lack of proportionality discussed at the beginning of this book is a stark obstacle to major forcible alterations of the status quo.

OBJECTIONS AND REBUTTALS

The position I have outlined is open to several lines of rebuttal, objection, and query. First, if perceptions of resolve are so important, how are they determined? What leads decision-makers to believe that their adversaries are willing to risk war over an issue? To what extent are reputations for high resolve or lack of it tied to particular states or statesmen as contrasted with being strongly influenced by specific situations? To what extent is the world seen as highly interconnected, with a state's behavior in one situation strongly influencing the way others expect him to behave under quite different circumstances? Many questionable policies have been justified in terms of the need to show resolve. The war in Vietnam is the most obvious example, but others are more recent. Thus, Brent Scowcroft argues that the deployment of the MX is necessary "to demonstrate U.S. national will and cohesion." The *Wall Street Journal* claims that the vote by the House of Representatives to terminate covert aid to the Nicaraguan rebels unless certain conditions are met "contributes to a world image of U.S. irresolution and weakness. If it stands in the Senate, Latins will have even more cause to wonder what, if anything, North Americans stand for. And people all around the world will be asking if this is still the country that once was willing to fight despotism." I think these arguments are farfetched and that resolve is tied to particular cases, but unfortunately our knowledge in this crucial area is limited.[15]

Objectives are likely to start from the fact that my general position, like the argument for assured destruction, denies that the details of the strategic balance matter because the incentives against starting a war are so strong. This immediately leads to two areas of contradiction. The first involves the stability-instability paradox, which I think has been exaggerated but which is still troublesome. If the balance of terror is robust, is there not a danger that the Soviet Union can exploit this stability? I have discussed this problem at length and need say no more about it here. Second, my argument, like many of the criticisms of the countervailing strategy, is a complacent one in implying that because the balance is stable, war is terribly unlikely. But how can this view be reconciled with the fear that current American policy could lead to war? George Kennan's argument illustrates the problem:

> The fragile nuclear balance that has prevailed in recent years is rapidly being undermined, not so much by the steady buildup of the nuclear arsenals on both sides (for they already represent nothing more than preposterous accumulations of overkill), but rather by technological advances that threaten to break down the verifiability of the respective capabilities and to stimulate the fears, the temptations, and the compulsions of a "first strike" mentality. We are getting very close that today.[16]

But the grounds for Kennan's alarmism seem shaky because the rest of his analysis implies that the balance is not fragile. If it were, would not the arguments of the countervailing strategy make a great deal of sense? Would not the United States have to meet the increase in Soviet military power and be prepared to fight a wide range of nuclear and conventional wars? On this point Bernard Brodie offered a consistent argument in the mid-1970s, holding that the strategic balance was so stable that the main objective of arms control—reducing the chance of war—was already met and that statesmen could therefore concentrate on the lesser objective of saving money.[17] I will argue below that even though the inhibitions against large-scale violence are so strong that even a foolish policy such as the countervailing strategy is not likely to lead to war, it indeed can increase the chance of this disaster.

[158]

A more troublesome objection is that there exists a potential for situations which could make the complacency unwarranted. One such difficulty has been noted: if the Russians were willing to run very high risks, they could challenge important Western interests. But although such an image of the Soviets would entail less optimistic conclusions than I hold, it is not clear that it would lead to the countervailing strategy. Even with this strategy in place, resisting Soviet advances would lead to the danger of escalation, a danger which, if the Soviets are very bold, they would be willing to run. Knowing this, would the United States dare stand firm? A second and related problem is that, even if the Russians are cautious, they might come to believe that the United States was so easy to coerce that infringements on its important interests were possible. There is no way to dismiss this danger, but I do not think it is hard for the United States to make it most unlikely. Indeed, I think it would be difficult to tempt the Soviets into doing something so rash as to attack Western Europe. But to at least a slight extent, this danger is increased by U.S. professions of weakness and denials of its ability to meet its obligations. At this point, however, the Russians seem quite skeptical of such statements. Perhaps they do not want to strengthen the proponents of the countervailing strategy by echoing these claims, but if in fact they were pressing hard to expand, it would be in their interest to reinforce the American doubts.

The third challenge to my position as too complacent is stronger. It is the product of four factors, some or all of which often coincide: proxies can be used for aggression; there are grey areas in which the status quo is not clear or not seen in the same way by both sides; disturbing events can occur without being stimulated by either superpower; and the status quo can be changed in stages. These circumstances make deterrence much more difficult. The status quo can be changed without the Soviets having to run high risks or, a greater danger, what they see as safe can lead to conflict that may not stay confined. The Korean and Vietnam wars are cases where Soviet forces were not employed; fighting in Angola, Ethiopia, and Afghanistan involved a confluence of these factors. To take the last case, although Afghanistan had been neutral, it is on the Soviet border and the Soviet security concerns there are greater than the American. The Russians gained their influence in two stages: the coup of April 1978, which occurred without their connivance and perhaps without their advance knowledge, and the invasion a year and a half later, which ratified the change in Afghanistan's position and can be seen as confirming the new status quo. Indeed, if plans had not misfired, Russian troops would have been invited into the country by the government and it would have been hard to term the move an invasion at all. Change in similar situations will surely continue. The status-quo powers do not have a great advantage in the bargaining that is involved; the Soviet role, at least in the early stages, is not necessarily great; the risks will often seem low and controllable. But I do not see this as a refutation of my argument. The major components of American military power surely cannot deal with all aspects of world politics. As Alexander George and Richard Smoke have stressed, one should not ask deterrence to substitute for foreign policy.[18] The countervailing strategy, even were it not defective, could not provide much assistance in these contingencies. Whether the problems created are important to the United States can be debated, but it is clear that they are largely beyond the scope of the policies we are concerned with here.

The final and most frequently advanced reason why my analysis could be too complacent is that deterrence must work under terrible stress as well as in ordinary circumstances. It is easy to deter the Soviets from launching a "bolt from the blue" attack against the United States and not hard to discourage an attack against Europe or the Persian Gulf as long as the international atmosphere is calm. But deterrence is harder in a crisis. While actual contingencies that might arise are hard to predict (before it happened, who would have thought of a Cuban missile crisis?), several possibilities are obvious: a revolt in East

[160]

Germany aided, once it was under way, by the Federal Republic; a civil war in Yugoslavia in which one faction invited the assistance of Soviet troops; a major Israeli-Syrian war; a large-scale Chinese attack on Vietnam leading to some sort of Soviet military action against China; a nuclear war between India and Pakistan. None of these cases requires the Soviet Union actively to seek opportunities to change the status quo; all of them present the Soviets with defensive as well as offensive incentives to use force because they raise the possibility that if the USSR does not act the situation might deteriorate badly; all could be more dangerous than any events which have yet occurred. The latter point perhaps offers some reason for hope—while we can imagine a lot of awful things, the fact that none of them has happened over a thirty-year period may show how unlikely they are. But it is hard to dismiss them on this ground. The question then remains of how the United States should be prepared to cope with them and, more specifically, of how military posture contributes to this endeavor. The lack of previous experience, the hypothetical nature of the cases, and their probable complexity rule out dogmatic assertions.

It is likely that American deterrence policy would play a larger role in these cases than it could in situations of the Afghanistan type. But here too other aspects of American foreign policy, particularly the state of Soviet-American relations, probably would be more important than the military forces and options available. (This is not to deny that American defense policy can influence the broader relationship with the Soviet Union.) Questions of overall policy toward the Soviets, important as they are, are beyond the scope of this book, and I would only note that those who support the countervailing strategy tend to favor a "hard-line" foreign policy, believing that the Soviets are quite expansionist, that firmness is required to contain the threat, and that the gravest danger is that they will underestimate American resolve. Those who take a position on defense policy similar to that outlined here usually see the Soviets as less aggressive and think that a policy which combines conciliation with a defense of Western interests can produce better relations.[19] But while military policy is linked to general foreign policy both logically and psychologically, the former is only a fairly small piece of the latter.

But even if military factors would not be the most important determinant of behavior in these kinds of situations, they could have some impact. Would the countervailing strategy deter the Russians from moving where they otherwise would have found American threats incredible? The basic argument of this book is that it would not. For the Russians to find the countervailing strategy's threats credible, they must think that the American leaders believe they can be implemented without leading to the destruction of American society. Credibility is largely a result of perceptions of risk and resolve. Being able to deny the Soviets a military advantage in a crisis is not more necessary for deterrence during a crisis than it is in calmer periods.

COSTS AND DANGERS OF THE COUNTERVAILING STRATEGY

Given the impossibility of proving most of these points, would it be better to err on the safe side and adopt the countervailing strategy? As I noted, it is much easier to show that the strategy is not necessary for deterrence than to show that it would not bolster it at least a bit. Several lines of reply are persuasive, however. Some of them are familiar and need only be listed. First, the monetary costs of the new weapons are not insignificant, especially in the current state of the American economy. Second, so far the strategy has alarmed more than it has reassured our European allies. Although, for reasons noted in chapter 2, it is not reasonable to expect any American policy to please them, one that is divisive weakens the alliance's internal ties and at least slightly decreases the credibility of the threats to run risks on Europe's behalf. Third, the Russians are likely to see current U.S. strategy as an attempt not only to contain them, but to menace their security. A cautious Russian leader could easily take the view that both the doctrine and the forces planned are aimed at providing a first-strike capability. As a result, I think, the chance for arms-control agreements and other mutually beneficial understandings is decreased. Although the projected buildup may have convinced the Russians to offer significant concessions if the United States would reciprocate, the strategy leads to the rejection of such bargains. The argument that current American defense policy diminishes chances for political settlement leads, of course, to the broader issues of how the United States can influence the Soviet Union, issues which, as we noted, are outside the scope of this analysis.

Fourth, espousing the countervailing strategy raises the risk that decision-makers will talk themselves into believing that high levels of conventional violence and even limited nuclear wars could be kept under control. This raises twin dangers. First, control may prove to be impossible. Earlier we noted the increased role of doctrine and beliefs in shaping behavior, but the belief that events can be controlled is only a necessary, and not a sufficient, condition for limited superpower wars. Furthermore, it is not at all clear that a world in which force was tamed in this way would be in the West's interests. While the danger of all-out war might be decreased, the way could be opened for the threat and use of force to change the status quo unless the West maintained both escalation dominance and the willingness to pay the price of wars which, while limited, would still be very costly.[20]

Probably more important than the direct costs and dangers of the countervailing strategy are the effects that stem from the strategy's conventionalized view of the ways in which force exercises influence in the nuclear era. First, by calling for escalation dominance and downplaying the extent to which any superpower crisis involves competition in risk-taking, American decision-makers both underestimate their overall ability to defend their interests in the face of Soviet-military strength and overestimate the ease with which they can prevail if they have the ability to deny the Soviets local military advantages. By implying that what is important is the ability to block military gains from limited adventures, the United States undercuts its own resolve to make a Soviet move in Europe or the Persian Gulf prohibitively risky. It implies that the Soviets could safely move where the local military balance favors them. While it is unlikely that the Russians believe they could, the U.S. might be more submissive than it needs to be.

George Kennan's point about the impact of the Soviet INF applies more widely: these forces "might conceivably serve as instruments of political intimidation; but it takes two to make a successful act of intimidation; and the very improbability of the actual use of these weapons means that no one in Western Europe needs to be greatly intimidated by them unless he wishes to be. Smaller powers than Germany and France have stood up, manfully and successfully, to threats more real than this one."21 If the American leaders convince themselves that deterrence is possible only if they deploy the forces called for in the strategy, and if those forces are not forthcoming or if the Soviets counterbalance them, then the American bargaining position will be harmed and American resolve weakened. If the forces are deployed, however, and the American leaders fool themselves into believing that they are now able safely to stand firm, they will not be in a strong position when a crisis reveals that the risks of escalation are still great. By missing the importance of the willingness to run risks, the strategy may leave the decision-makers psychologically ill equipped to deal with confrontations that starkly reveal the inability of even an excellent military position to ensure security.

The countervailing strategy thus contributes to, and perhaps springs from, the American tendency to shoot ourselves in the foot by creating unnecessary problems that require great efforts to dispel. That was the case, for instance, with the "window of vulnerability," and as this example brings out, two additional factors, both very hard to control, feed this tendency. One is the domestic political debate. The party out of power has strong incentives to find supposed weaknesses in existing policy. If the incumbent is defeated, the new government also will need to differentiate its policy from that of its discredited predecessor. Second, the nature of their profession drives defense analysts to conjure up new dangers, new strategies, and new options. When that tendency is combined with the understandable desire on the part of the military to be able to fight as well as possible if war comes, the result is lengthened lists of Soviet targets that need to be destroyed, ever-increasing requirements for deterrence, and a series of new obstacles that we think must be surmounted to protect our vital interests.

The second general cost of the countervailing strategy is that, by stressing that war could result from the Soviet calculation that the balance of forces permits military adventures, it is likely to exacerbate what is probably a greater danger: that the Soviet Union might become desperate because of internal or external pressures and come to see war as either necessary or inevitable. When states are pushed hard enough, they may go to war when a rational analysis would indicate that the step is disastrous.[22] And if decision-makers believe that war will come no matter what they do, pressures for a preemptive strike are strong. In the current era this is especially true because a "decapitation" strike against leadership and C^3 offers the only possible way to cripple the other's capacity for retaliation. Even if this is impossible, such an attack would almost surely disrupt the other side's response, a matter of relatively little importance if the war is unrestrained, but very significant if a controlled counterforce war is foreseen, as in the countervailing strategy.[23] Furthermore, Soviet doctrine stresses the advantages of striking first.

All the arguments about deterrence—both those of the countervailing strategy and the ones made here—involve convincing the other side that war will result if it takes the prohibited action and that the result will be worse than remaining at peace. Implicitly then, deterrence also involves the promise that war will not break out if the other cooperates.[24] When this promise is

[165]

shattered, when the other believes that war will come no matter what it does, then deterrence cannot work. So it is not surprising that one expert argues that "the sole contingency which could persuade any Soviet leadership of the 'rationality' of nuclear war in pursuit of policy would be the unassailable, incontrovertible, dire evidence that the United States was about to strike the Soviet Union."[25] It is hard to say exactly what could make the Russians believe that war was inevitable, and here again the general state of Soviet-American relations would be more important than the military doctrine the United States adopted. But gaining escalation dominance would not reduce the danger and might contribute to a Soviet sense of being cornered.

Measures to show that the United States is willing to stand firm to protect its interests must, accordingly, be coupled with demonstrated willingness to leave the Soviet Union secure in its vital interests. The Soviets need to be convinced not only that expansion is too risky to attempt, but also that the opposite course will not lead to increased U.S. pressures. It would be very dangerous if either side believed that concessions would only lead to a delayed show-down, one in which it would be at a greater disadvantage. To put the same point more generally: while it is hard to imagine the Russians running significant risks to their homeland in order to expand, this does not eliminate the possibility of their taking risks. They would be likely to do so were they to believe that this was the best, if not the only, way to protect themselves. Being conciliatory toward the West could appear more likely to produce a war than would taking a firm stand.[26] Attempts by either superpower to show how tough it is will be dangerous if they lead the other side to infer that if its rival prevails in one crisis it will later seek to menace the other state's security.

This danger would also complicate attempts to terminate a nuclear or large conventional war. Since neither side could be defeated in the traditional sense, each would have to be reassured that the other was not merely looking for a short truce, which it would break when conditions were propitious. As I noted earlier, in nuclear peace-making the ability to make credible promises is as important as the ability to make credible threats.

GUIDELINES FOR POLICY

Going beyond these negative admonitions is not easy, and I cannot provide as much guidance for the working out of a realistic policy as I would like. An adequate policy must start with the realization that the nuclear revolution calls for ways of thinking and courses of action quite different from those appropriate to earlier eras. Because all-out war would be a catastrophe for both sides, competition in risk-taking now has a central place in bargaining and deterrence. This means that confrontations and limited wars between the superpowers will serve primarily as generators of risk. In a crisis or to respond to a major Soviet provocation, the United States certainly needs alternatives to passivity or an all-out strike. But it has had them for at least twenty years. The missiles need not be fired all at once. The common claim that an American president might be left with only the choice between humiliation and holocaust is silly. If the C^3 system survives, there are any number of actions that can be taken to increase the costs to the Soviets and the risks to both sides.

The targets the United States would want to hit would probably be military ones, but pressure would not be brought to bear through the traditional route of gaining military advantage. Instead, the strikes would both demonstrate resolve and generate risks that further escalation will occur. The debate about whether U.S. war plans do or should call for "demonstration attacks"[27] misses the essential point that any limited nuclear strikes will have this function even if it was not their purpose. As long as the societies of both sides are vulnerable, a crisis or a limited superpower war will be like the game of Chicken. Resolve and judgments of the other's resolve are as crucial to war-fighting as to deterrence. Since we are dealing with probabilities of all-out war rather than with firm decisions to produce this outcome, some of the proportionality between means and ends that nuclear weapons destroyed is restored. Just as in the past some objectives were worth a war because the damage from the conflict was less than the expected gains, so now some objectives are worth a risk—albeit a low one—of total destruction.[28]

While the existence of nuclear weapons is essential to this strategy, their use is not. It is the combination of the suicidal nature of all-out war and the Russians' understanding that crises generate threats that leave something to chance which produces the dynamics discussed above. But the Russians reject the notion that limited nuclear wars could be used to demonstrate resolve and usefully increase risks. I see no reason for the United States to try to disabuse them. Our limited nuclear options should be retained, but regarded as something which might have utility only in the future, if the Soviet view changes. American policy should not be built around these options; decision-makers should not pretend that the security of American interests depends on them, and indeed we should talk about them as little as possible.

The most obvious requirement for American nuclear forces is that they provide the unquestioned ability to destroy the Soviet Union even if the Soviets stage a skillful first strike. As most analysts have pointed out, it is harder to develop adequate C^3 for this mission than it is to supply the forces themselves. Even more difficult is the task of ensuring that the top decision-makers would not all be killed by a Soviet attack. Evacuation plans for them should be improved and practices should be frequent, both to make success more likely in the event of an actual attack and to accustom the Russians to the idea. Were the first occasion on which the leadership moved from Washington a severe crisis, the Soviets might think that war was inevitable. This danger also shows the value of forces which are relatively invulnerable on a day-to-day basis. If forces are hard to destroy

[168]

only when they are alerted during a crisis and go into what is known as a "generated" state, they must either move to alert status early in a crisis or risk the danger—admittedly very small—that the Russians would preempt before they were generated.[29]

If crises and local disputes function as generators of risk, American conventional forces need not be required to beat back a large-scale attack. But they must be sufficient to deal with smaller probes and prevent the quick seizure of important territory. If the aggressor can complete his adventure before the defender can react, he can establish a new status quo from which he can be dislodged only with difficulty. George and Smoke found that deterrent threats are often ineffective against faits accomplis.[30] If the Soviets could expect to conquer Western Europe quickly, the danger of their trying would be much greater than if they thought that although they could win, the campaign would be prolonged. In the former case, the risk might be seen as relatively low because victory could come before the fighting had a chance to spread. Whether the Soviets could win a quick victory has been debated,[31] but the point here is that it is important to ensure that they could not expect such an outcome. This argument, like many others, indicates the great value of constructing strong fortifications along the inter-German border, a move that German domestic politics renders extremely difficult. Even if this cannot be done, there is great merit in Secretary Brown's argument that "what is needed to increase the assurance of deterrence . . . is to increase the capability that the NATO allies have to . . . hold off the Soviet Warsaw Pact forces during the first few days and first few weeks of an attack."[32] Similarly, in the Persian Gulf the objective of the Rapid Deployment Force need not be to provide a full defense against a large Soviet attack. What is more important is to be able to get into place quickly, to create an unambiguous American commitment, to force the Soviet troops into prolonged combat with American soldiers, and so to create a situation that the Russians know will be very dangerous.[33] The Sovi-

[169]

ets must not be allowed to believe that a major challenge can be conducted in a way in which they can keep control of the risks.

Too often discussions of defense policy are couched in terms of the need to deal with extremely dangerous situations without sufficient attention to how our policies can make those situations less likely. Although some confrontations are likely to be inevitable, political understandings with the Soviet Union may minimize their frequency and danger. The danger in these conflicts will not completely disappear, however, and developing more military options is not likely to make them easier to cope with. We cannot escape the element of risk. Clausewitz remarked: "Kind-hearted people might . . . think there was some ingenious way to disarm or defeat an enemy without too much bloodshed, and might imagine this is the true goal of the art of war. Pleasant as it sounds, it is a fallacy that must be exposed."[34] In the nuclear era, this is as true for the running of risks as it is for the actual spending of blood and treasure.

I began this book by arguing that no nuclear strategy can be fully rational. Making use of the risk of war not only restores some proportionality, it also restores some rationality. But only some. There is something horribly irrational about a strategy which turns on the inherently uncertain possibility of unleashing the destruction that everyone wants above all to avoid. But without defenses that would repeal the nuclear revolution, this possibility cannot be excised. The countervailing strategy fails because it tries to escape from the resulting dilemmas. But if the realization that one must build a strategy on the risks and uncertainties inherent in nuclear bargaining can avoid many of the errors and dangers of current policy, it cannot bring back the rational relationship between force and foreign policy that previously existed. We will have to find new and different paths. G. K. Chesterton said, "I have seen the truth and it makes no sense." I do not claim that the arguments I have made here are the truth. But I do think that nuclear weapons have so changed our world that much of the truth does not make sense.

Notes

1. Robert McNamara, "The Military Role of Nuclear Weapons," *Foreign Affairs*, 62 (Fall 1983), 68.

1. The Nuclear Revolution

1. The most complete discussion of pre-1960 war plans is David Rosenberg, "The Origins of Overkill: Nuclear Weapons and American Strategy, 1945–1960," *International Security*, 7 (Spring 1983), 3–71. For a briefer and more general treatment, see Aaron Friedberg, "A History of the U.S. Strategic 'Doctrine'—1945 to 1980," *Journal of Strategic Studies*, 3 (December 1980), 37–71. The distinction between deterrence by punishment and deterrence by denial is developed in Glenn Snyder, *Deterrence and Defense* (Princeton: Princeton University Press, 1961), pp. 14–16.

2. For discussions of the security dilemma, see Herbert Butterfield, *History and Human Relations* (London: Collins, 1951), pp. 9–36; John Herz, "Idealist Internationalism and the Security Dilemma," *World Politics*, 2 (January 1950), 157–80; Arnold Wolfers, *Discord and Collaboration* (Baltimore: Johns Hopkins University Press, 1962), pp. 81–102; and Robert Jervis, "Cooperation under the Security Dilemma," *World Politics*, 30 (January 1978), 167–214.

3. Thomas Schelling, "Comment," in Klaus Knorr and Thornton Read, eds., *Limited Strategic War*, (New York: Praeger, 1962), p. 255.

4. Bernard Brodie's essays in *The Absolute Weapon* (New York: Harcourt Brace, 1946) were amazingly prescient in grasping this. For an excellent recent treatment, see Michael Mandelbaum, *The Nuclear Revolution* (New York: Cambridge University Press, 1981). As John Herz showed, these changes could have been produced without nuclear weapons. What is required is the ability to inflict extreme pain on the other side without first destroying its

armies. See "The Rise and Demise of the Territorial State," *World Politics*, 9 (July 1957), 473–93.

5. *Foreign Relations of the United States, 1950,* vol. 1, *National Security Affairs; Foreign Economic Policy* (Washington, D.C.: Government Printing Office, 1977), p. 39. Kennan's discussion of this memorandum appears in his *Memoirs*, vol. 1 (Boston: Little, Brown, 1967), pp. 471–76.

6. A useful distinction here is that between fate control and behavior control developed in John Thibaut and Harold Kelley, *The Social Psychology of Groups* (New York: Wiley, 1959), pp. 107–28.

7. David Rosenberg, "U.S. Nuclear Stockpile, 1945 to 1950," *Bulletin of the Atomic Scientists*, 38 (May 1982), 25–30. For an excellent discussion of the early war plans, see Rosenberg, "The Origins of Overkill," pp. 4–18.

8. The relevant document, NSC-30, "United States Policy on Atomic Warfare," is printed in *Foreign Relations of the United States, 1948,* vol. 1, part 2, *General; The United Nations* (Washington, D.C.: Government Printing Office, 1976), pp. 624–28.

9. The first phrase comes from the Basic National Security Policy of 1956, quoted in David Rosenberg, "'A Smoking Radiating Ruin at the End of Two Hours': Documents on American Plans for Nuclear War with the Soviet Union, 1945–55," *International Security*, 6 (Winter 1981/1982), 14; the second is from NSC 162/2 in *The Pentagon Papers* (Senator Gravel edition; Boston: Beacon, 1971), 1: 426.

10. The best treatment is Rosemary Foot, *The Wrong War* (forthcoming).

11. Bernard Brodie, *War and Politics* (New York: Macmillan, 1973), pp. 1–28. As Hans Morgenthau put it: "The very conceptions of nuclear 'weapons' and of nuclear 'war' are misnomers. For when we speak of weapons, we have in mind a rational relationship between a means, an instrument and an end": "The Fallacy of Thinking Conventionally about Nuclear Weapons," in David Carlton and Carlo Schaerf, eds., *Arms Control and Technological Innovation* (New York: Wiley, 1976), p. 255. Also see Morgenthau, "The Four Paradoxes of Nuclear Strategy," *American Political Science Review*, 58 (March 1964), 25–35, and Morgenthau et al., "Western Values and Total War," *Commentary*, 32 (October 1961), 280.

12. The phrase comes from what one military observer expected of a somewhat later war plan. See Rosenberg, "'A Smoking Radiating Ruin at the End of Two Hours.'"

13. *Foreign Relations of the United States, 1948,* vol. 1, part 2, pp. 663–69. The war aims were revised in 1954 and presented in NSC 5410/1. See Rosenberg, "'A Smoking Radiating Ruin at the End of Two Hours,'" p. 29.

14. Quoted in David Lilienthal, *The Journals of David E. Lilienthal*, vol. 2 (New York: Harper & Row, 1964), p. 391.

15. Morgenthau, "The Four Paradoxes of Nuclear Strategy," p. 35. Morgenthau's rejection of Realism is further developed in his "World Politics and the Politics of Oil," in Gary Eppen, ed., *Energy: the Policy Issues* (Chicago: University of Chicago Press, 1975), pp. 43–51.

16. George Kennan, "On Nuclear War," *New York Review of Books*, January

21, 1982, p. 8. For further discussion, see Kennan, *The Nuclear Delusion* (New York: Pantheon, 1983), pp. xxviii–xxix.

17. For good discussions, see Thomas Schelling, *Arms and Influence* (New Haven: Yale University Press, 1966), pp. 1–34, and Snyder, *Deterrence and Defense*, pp. 3–51.

18. The remark was made by Lord Chatham on the eve of the American Revolution, quoted in Robert W. Tucker and David Hendrickson, *The Fall of the First British Empire* (Baltimore: Johns Hopkins University Press, 1982), pp. 400–401. Also see L. L. Farrar, Jr., *Arrogance and Anxiety: The Ambivalence of German Power, 1848–1914* (Iowa City: University of Iowa Press, 1981), p. 182. Of course, such views can be wrong, as Chatham's was.

19. John Mueller, "The Search for the Single 'Breaking Point' in Vietnam: The Statistics of a Deadly Quarrel," *International Studies Quarterly*, 24 (December 1980), 497–519. Also see the literature cited in note 16, chapter 5. The costs were borne over an extended period of time and presumably only the prospective ones, not those already paid, were considered when deciding whether to continue fighting. Perhaps the North would not have entered the war had it known how much punishment it would have to absorb.

20. Michael Howard, *The Franco-Prussian War* (New York: Collier, 1969), pp. 273–75.

21. Henry Kissinger, *Years of Upheaval* (Boston: Little, Brown, 1982), p. 273; Department of Defense, *Annual Report, F.Y. 1980* (Washington, D.C.: Government Printing Office, 1979), p. 64.

22. Office of Technology Assessment of the Congress of the United States, *The Effects of Nuclear War* (Washington, D.C.: Office of Technology Assessment, 1979), pp. 112–15; R. P. Turco, et al., "Nuclear Winter: Global Consequences of Multiple Nuclear Explosions," *Science*, 222 (December 23, 1983), 1283–92; Paul Ehrlich, "Long-Term Biological Consequences of Nuclear War," ibid., 1293–300. A nontechnical version of the findings presented in the latter two articles is Carl Sagan, "Nuclear War and Climatic Catastrophe," *Foreign Affairs*, 62 (Winter 1983/84), 257–92. The "nuclear winter" effect is produced by the soot from burning cities and therefore would be greatly attenuated in a purely counterforce attack.

23. Glenn Snyder, "The Balance of Power and the Balance of Terror" in Paul Seabury, ed., *The Balance of Power* (San Francisco: Chandler, 1965).

24. Brodie, *War and Politics*, pp. 425–26.

25. Ibid., p. 426, emphasis omitted. Of course, the strategic balance was not terribly stable at that time because the Russians did not clearly possess a second-strike capability. Also note the odd congeries of beliefs: those like Brodie who see the strategic balance as robust (ibid., p. 380) also tended to downplay the significance of the stability-instability paradox, whereas those who see the balance as more delicate focus more on the dangers of limited Soviet adventures. Some links between these beliefs are provided by the respective images of the Soviet Union. For a further discussion, see below, pp. 26, 61–63, 156–57.

26. Coit Blacker, "The Kremlin and Detente: Soviet Conceptions, Hopes,

and Expectations," in Alexander George, *Managing U.S.–Soviet Rivalry* (Boulder, Colo.: Westview, 1983), pp. 127–28.

27. Thomas Schelling, *The Strategy of Conflict* (Cambridge: Harvard University Press, 1960), and Schelling, *Arms and Influence*.

28. H. Robert Haldeman, *The Ends of Power* (New York: New York Times Book Co., 1968), pp. 82–83, 98.

29. DoD, *Annual Report, F.Y. 1979* (Washington, D.C.: Government Printing Office, 1978), p. 54. Emphasis added.

30. For further discussion, see Schelling, *Arms and Influence*, pp. 99, 114 and chapter 5, below.

31. U.S. House of Representatives, Committee on Armed Services, *Hearings on Military Posture*, part 1, 93d Cong., 2d sess. (Washington, D.C.: Government Printing Office, 1974), p. 49. Also see Schlesinger's testimony in U.S. Senate, Subcommittee on Arms Control, International Law and Organization of the Committee on Foreign Relations, *Briefing on Counterforce Attacks*, 93d Cong., 2d sess. (Washington, D.C.: Government Printing Office, 1975), p. 44.

32. Quoted in U.S. Senate, Committee on Foreign Relations, *Hearing on Presidential Directive 59*, 96th Cong. 2d sess., September 16, 1980 (Washington, D.C.: Government Printing Office, 1981), p. 7. See also Kissinger's argument in his interview in *The Economist*, February 3, 1979, p. 18: "I believe that the side whose only strategic option is to target the civilian population and industrial capacity of its opponent and which can define no military objective will be relying on a strategy that will be psychologically and politically almost untenable—especially if it is also inferior in forces for local intervention. . . . [O]ur retaliatory capability is enormous but if the only probable targets are civilians it will nevertheless leave us politically paralyzed." Also see Kissinger, *The White House Years*, (Boston: Little Brown, 1979), pp. 217–18.

33. DoD, *Annual Report, F.Y. 1984* (Washington, D.C.: Government Printing Office, 1983), p. 52.

34. Indeed, to use Schelling's terminology, states were issuing warnings, not threats. See *Strategy of Conflict*, pp. 123–24.

35. U.S. House of Representatives, Armed Services Committee, *Hearings on H.R. 2287, Department of Defense Authorization for F.Y. 1984*, 98th Cong. 1st sess. (Washington, D.C.: Government Printing Office, 1983), p. 113.

36. Fred Kaplan, *The Wizards of Armageddon* (New York: Simon & Schuster, 1983), p. 371.

37. Of course, nuclear weapons have not changed everything. For good studies of deterrence without nuclear weapons which provide some relevant evidences, see George Quester, *Deterrence before Hiroshima* (New York: Wiley, 1966) and Glenn Snyder and Paul Diesing, *Conflict among Nations* (Princeton: Princeton University Press, 1977).

38. An excellent analysis of why these beliefs were held is Jack Snyder, *The Ideology of the Offensive: Military Decision Making and the Disasters of 1914* (Ithaca: Cornell University Press, 1984).

39. For elaboration of this point, see Robert Jervis, "Deterrence and Perception," *International Security*, 7 (Winter 1982/1983), 14–19.

40. Bernard Brodie, "The Development of Nuclear Strategy, *International Security*, 2 (Spring 1978), 82.

41. Henry Kissinger, *Nuclear Weapons and Foreign Policy* (New York: Harper, 1957), p. 438,

42. The vulnerability of command, control, and communications systems means that this statement may be exaggerated. See below, pp. 119–20, 165.

43. Henry Kissinger, "NATO: The Next Thirty Years," *Survival*, 21 (November/December, 1979), 267.

44. Kissinger, *Years of Upheaval*, p. 999. Also see his "NATO Defense and the Soviet Threat," *Survival*, 21 (November/December 1979), 265–67. This is also Colin Gray's position. See, for example, "Targeting Problems for Central War," *Naval War College Review*, 33 (January-February 1980), 4.

45. For claims to the contrary, see James Schlesinger's testimony in *Hearings on Military Posture*, pp. 46, 49; Colin Gray, "The MX Debate," *Survival*, 20 (May/June 1978), 111; "Targeting Problems for Central War," p. 4.

46. The questions of why compellence is more difficult than deterrence, and under what conditions this is true, are still far from being completely answered. For further discussion, see below, pp. 153–55.

47. Herman Kahn, *On Thermonuclear War* (Princeton: Princeton University Press, 1960), pp. 126–44. As Kahn has pointed out, if the United States thought that after a first-strike on the Soviet Union, the Soviets could retaliate and cause, say 20 million casualties, this would not be sufficient damage limitation for a first-strike capability, but might be sufficient to make credible the threat of striking in response to a Soviet attack on Europe. In other words, the United States could prefer the status quo to a war in which 20 million Americans died and prefer the latter outcome to seeing Russia conquer Europe. To use Kahn's terminology, the United States would have Type II deterrence without infringing on Russia's Type I deterrence. Similarly, some analysts have justified the MX in terms of its ability to present a credible threat of a counterforce strike in response to an invasion of Europe even though the USSR's retaliatory ability would be great enough so that Soviet leaders would not fear an unprovoked U.S. attack. (See, for example, Morton Kaplan, "What the MX Would Do," *Washington Times*, April 29, 1983.) But in practice estimates of war outcomes are far too rough and uncertain to allow this kind of precision. McNamara's attempt to gain sufficient damage limitation to make U.S. threats to defend Europe credible, but not too much to reach a first-strike capability, was similarly flawed. One result was the difficulty in restraining the Air Force's call for trying to maintain the ability to launch a disarming first strike. See McNamara's 1962 memorandum printed in Robert Scheer, *With Enough Shovels: Reagan, Bush, and Nuclear War* (New York: Random House, 1982), p. 150. An implication of James McConnell's analysis is that the USSR is seeking Type II deterrence without necessarily trying to deny the United States a second-strike capability: *Soviet and American Strategic Doctrines: One More Time* (Alexandria, Va.: Center for Naval Analyses, January 1980), Professional Paper 271.

[175]

2. *Tensions and Attempted Escapes*

1. Bernard Brodie, *War and Politics* (New York: Macmillan, 1973), pp. 430–1.

2. For a related argument, see Patrick Morgan, *Deterrence* (Beverly Hills, Calif.: Sage, 1977), pp. 90–124.

3. This trade-off is discussed by Thomas Schelling, *The Strategy of Conflict* (Cambridge: Harvard University Press, 1960) and Glenn Synder, *Deterrence and Defense* (Princeton: Princeton University Press, 1961). The countervailing strategy tries to escape from this tension the same way it seeks implementable options: by calling for the ability to destroy Russian military targets and denying the Soviets military advantage from their actions. But this does not deal with the essential problem, as I show in chapter 5 below.

4. Jervis, *Perception and Misperception in International Politics* (Princeton: Princeton University Press, 1976), pp. 128–42.

5. Henry Kissinger, *Nuclear Weapons and Foreign Policy* (New York: Harper, 1957), p. 185. Kissinger has changed his view and now argues that while nuclear war might be kept restrained, "in all likelihood, the problem of limiting the use of [nuclear] weapons . . . will find no acceptable theoretical formulation in advance: as a practical matter, failure to achieve a consensus over a period of thirty years is a pretty good working definition of the impossibility of developing in the abstract a strategy of limited nuclear war": "Nuclear Weapons and the Peace Movement," *Washington Quarterly*, 5 (Summer 1982), 34.

6. *Foreign Relations of the United States, 1950*, vol. 1, *National Security Affairs; Foreign Economic Policy* (Washington, D.C.: Government Printing Office, 1977), pp. 29–30. See also Kennan's letter quoted in Herbert York, *The Advisors: Oppenheimer, Teller, and the Superbomb* (San Francisco: Freeman, 1976), p. 112, and McGeorge Bundy, "The Nature of Strategic Deterrence," *Survival*, 21 (November/December 1979), 268–73.

7. Quoted in *The Journals of David E. Lilienthal*, vol. 2 (New York: Harper & Row, 1964), pp. 466–473.

8. Kissinger, *Nuclear Weapons and Foreign Policy*, p. 160. Kissinger's inconsistency on this point is noted by William W. Kaufmann, "The Crisis in Military Affairs," *World Politics*, 10 (July 1958), 586–87.

9. Quoted in John Gaddis, *Strategies of Containment* (New York: Oxford University Press, 1968), pp. 167–68; see also p. 173.

10. Bernard Brodie, "AFAG Talk: Political Impact of U.S. Force Postures," May 28, 1963, pp. 6–7, in *Fourteen Informal Writings from the Unpublished Work of Bernard Brodie, 1952–1965*, (Santa Monica, Calif.: RAND, n.d.); *War and Politics*, p. 426.

11. *Report of the President's Commission on Strategic Forces*, April 6, 1983. Whatever explains this reversal, it is startling that the policy-making elite, mass media, and general public accepted it with so little questioning and resentment of those experts who suddenly, and with little embarrassment, admitted to have given misleading advice on a crucial issue over many years.

12. Richard Garwin, "The National Security and Next-Generation Strategic Forces," talk to the Chicago Council on Foreign Relations, September 1980, p. 10. It is often claimed that the ICBMs are particularly valuable because of

their ability to destroy hardened Soviet targets quickly. But the need for speed in a counterforce second strike has not been demonstrated. See below, pp. 114–15.

13. An excellent treatment of the escapes that were popular in the first years of the nuclear era is Bernard Brodie, *Strategy in the Missile Age* (Princeton: Princeton University Press, 1959), pp. 223–63.

14. "Transcript of Press Interview with President at White House," *New York Times*, March 30, 1983. A similar response can be produced by fear of war as well as by fear of the Soviet Union. The former—which can generate responses other than support for defense—can spring from negative evaluations of American policy or a pessimistic analysis of the ability of human beings in general to deal with nuclear weapons. If one thinks that war is likely, for any reason, the pressures to move away from a situation of mutual vulnerability are very great.

15. Hans Morgenthau, "The Fallacy of Thinking Conventionally about Nuclear Weapons," in David Carlton and Carlo Schaerf, eds., *Arms Control and Technological Innovation* (New York: Wiley, 1976), pp. 256–64. Under President Eisenhower, tactical nuclear weapons were sometimes referred to as "conventional." See the quotations in Fred Kaplan, *The Wizards of Armageddon* (New York: Simon & Schuster, 1983), p. 181; Fred Iklé, "Arms Control and National Defense," in Peter Duigan and Alvin Rabushaka, eds., *The United States in the 1980s* (Stanford: Hoover Institution Press, 1980), p. 427; and *The Foreign Relations of the United States: 1952–1954*, as quoted in Bernard Gwertzman, "Nuclear Arms: A Cool, Candid Debate," *New York Times*, July 14, 1983.

16. U.S. House of Representatives, Committee on Armed Services, *Hearings on Military Posture*, part 1, 93d Cong., 2d sess. (Washington, D.C.: Government Printing Office, 1974), p. 49; the Ann Arbor speech is quoted in William W. Kaufmann, *The McNamara Strategy* (New York: Harper & Row, 1964), p. 116. Of course, McNamara soon changed his position.

17. Paul Nitze, "Atoms, Strategy and Policy," *Foreign Affairs*, 34 (January 1956), 190–91.

18. Paul Nitze, "Is SALT II a Fair Deal for the United States?," (Washington, D.C.: Committee on the Present Danger, 1979), p. 6.

19. For a further discussion, see Robert Jervis, "Why Nuclear Superiority Doesn't Matter," *Political Science Quarterly*, 94 (Winter 1979–80), 617–33. Also see below, pp. 136–37.

20. This is slightly different from Herman Kahn's definition in *On Escalation* (Baltimore: Penguin, 1968), p. 290. See also U.S. Senate, Committee on Appropriations, *Hearings on S. Con. Res. 26*, 98th Cong., 1st sess. (Washington, D.C.: Government Printing Office, 1983), p. 231

21. See, for example, Weinberger's statement in Department of Defense, *Annual Report, F.Y. 1984* (Washington, D.C.: Government Printing Office, 1983), p. 57.

22. As William T. R. Fox put it, "When dealing with the absolute weapon, arguments based on relative advantage lose their point": "International Control of Atomic Weapons," in Bernard Brodie, ed., *The Absolute Weapon* (New York: Harcourt Brace, 1946), p. 181. See also Brodie's essays in that volume,

pp. 48, 75. The point is also well made in Kenneth Waltz, *The Spread of Nuclear Weapons: More May Be Better*, Adelphi Paper No. 171 (London: International Institute for Strategic Studies, 1981).

23. DoD, *Annual Report, F.Y. 1982* (Washington, D.C.: Government Printing Office, 1981), p. 41. Further difficulties with this line of argument are discussed below, pp. 127–29, 135–40.

24. For good discussions see Thomas Brown, "Number Mysticism, Rationality, and the Strategic Balance," *Orbis*, 21 (Fall 1977), 479–96, and William Baugh, *The Politics of Nuclear Balance* (New York and London: Longman, 1984), pp. 122–55, 166–77. I have discussed this problem at greater length in "The Drunkard's Search," unpublished manuscript.

25. Military leaders have a general bias in favor of the offensive, however. See Barry Posen, *The Sources of Military Doctrine: France, Britain, and Germany between the World Wars* (Ithaca: Cornell University Press, 1984), and Jack Snyder, *The Ideology of the Offensive: Military Decision Making and the Disasters of 1914* (Ithaca: Cornell University Press, 1984).

26. U.S. House of Representatives, Subcommittee on Department of Defense, *Appropriations for the F.Y. 1973 Defense Budget and F.Y. 1973–1977 Program*, 92d Cong., 2d sess., February 22, 1972, p. 65; U.S. Senate, Committee on Armed Services, *Hearings on F.Y. 1978 Military Procurement, Research and Development, and Personnel Strengths*, part 2, 95th Cong., 1st sess. (Washington, D.C.: Government Printing Office, 1977), p. 892; U.S. Senate, Preparedness Investigating Subcommittee of the Committee on Armed Services, *Hearings on Status of U.S. Strategic Power*, 90th Cong., 2d sess., April 30, 1968 (Washington, D.C.: Government Printing Office, 1968), p. 186; Francis Hoeber, "How Little Is Enough?," *International Security*, 3 (Winter 1978/1979), 67; Nitze, "Atoms, Strategy and Policy," pp. 190–91. Also see Colin Gray, "Nuclear Strategy: A Case for a Theory of Victory," *International Security*, 4 (Summer 1979), 66–67, 76–77. Even George Kennan argued that the United States should ensure that "if cataclysm is unavoidable, [the catastophe] is at least less than that suffered by our enemies." (*Foreign Relations of the United States, 1950*, vol. 1, p. 37.)

27. Quoted in Fred Greenstein, *The Hidden-Hand Presidency* (New York: Basic Books, 1982), p. 47.

28. See Hannes Adomeit, *Soviet Risk-Taking and Crisis Behavior* (London: Allen & Unwin, 1982); Jan Triska and David Finley, *Soviet Foreign Policy* (New York: Macmillan, 1968), pp. 310–49; Benjamin Lambeth, "Uncertainties for the Soviet War Planner," *International Security*, 7 (Winter 1982–1983), 141–44; Dennis Ross, "Risk Aversion in Soviet Decision-Making," in Jiri Valenta and William Potter, eds., *Soviet National Security Decision-Making* (London: Allen & Unwin, 1984).

3. *The Countervailing Strategy and Its Areas of Incoherence*

1. For accounts of the Reagan administration's position, see the stories by Richard Halloran in the *New York Times*, May 30, June 21, August 9, and

August 24, 1982, which are based on leaks from the five-year Defense Guidance; Michael Getler, "Administration's Nuclear War Policy Stance Still Murky," *Washington Post*, November 10, 1982; and the comments below, p. 70.

2. Excellent discussions are David Rosenberg, "The Origins of Overkill: Nuclear Weapons and American Strategy, 1945–1960," *International Security*, 7 (Spring 1983), 4–71; Desmond Ball, "U.S. Strategic Forces: How Would They Be Used?," ibid., 7 (Winter 1982/1983), 31–60; Ball, *Déjà vu: The Return to Counterforce in the Nixon Administration* (Santa Monica: California Seminar on Arms Control and Foreign Policy, December 1974); Ball, *Developments in U.S. Strategic Nuclear Policy under the Carter Administration*, ACIS Working Paper, No. 21 (Los Angeles: Center for International and Strategic Affairs, UCLA, February, 1980).

3. Statesmen generally see in such behavior indications of a Machiavellian and hostile plan. See Jervis, *Perception and Misperception in International Politics* (Princeton: Princeton University Press, 1976), pp. 319–42. John Erickson argues that the Soviet perceptions of the discrepancy between American declarations and war plans fit this pattern: "The Soviet View of Deterrence," *Survival*, 24 (November/December 1982), 242–51.

4. This belief is shared by many analysts who reject the countervailing strategy. See, for example, Robert McNamara, "The Military Role of Nuclear Weapons," *Foreign Affairs*, 62 (Fall 1983), 59–80. Chapter 5 explains why I think it is fundamentally erroneous.

5. There is some similarity between this doctrine and W. Ross Ashby's argument that for a system to be stable the variety in the disturbance must be matched by the variety in the regulator: *Introduction to Cybernetics* (London: Chapman & Hall, 1961), pp. 202–18. This concept has been used in a way that is interesting but flawed in Richard Rosecrance, *Action and Reaction in World Politics* (Boston: Little, Brown, 1963).

6. U.S. Senate, Committee on Armed Services, *Hearings on Department of Defense Authorization for Appropriations for Fiscal Year 1984*, part 1, 98th Cong., 1st sess., February 1, 1983 (Washington, D.C.: Government Printing Office, 1983), p. 32; also see pp. 74, 101–2.

7. Zbigniew Brzezinski, "Remarks at Twenty-fifth Anniversary Assembly of the Atlantic Treaty Organization," Department of State, October 10, 1979, p. 4; Alexander Haig, "Peace and Deterrence," April 6, 1982 (U.S. Department of State, *Current Policy* No. 383), p. 3.

8. U.S. House of Representatives, Committee on Armed Services, *Hearings on H.R. 8390 and Review of the State of U.S. Strategic Forces*, 95th Cong., 1st sess. (Washington, D.C.: Government Printing Office, 1977), p. 162.

9. See the discussion in note 47, chapter 1.

10. Anthony Cordesman suggests that some of the stress on hitting OMT may have derived from the increasing number of warheads available to the United States in the 1970s: *Deterrence in the 1980s; Part I—American Strategic Forces and Extended Deterrence*, Adelphi Paper No. 175 (London: International Institute for Strategic Studies, Summer 1982), pp. 12–13. Like so many aspects of current doctrine, this is not entirely new. In 1950, one of the three categories

of targets was those deemed to retard Soviet advances into Western Europe: see David Rosenberg, " 'A Smoking Radiating Ruin at the End of Two Hours': Documents on American Plans for Nuclear War with the Soviet Union, 1945–55," *International Security,* 6 (Winter 1981/1982), pp. 9–11; also see Rosenberg, "American Atomic Strategy and the Hydrogen Bomb Decision," *Journal of American History,* 66 (June 1979), 74, and Rosenberg, "The Origins of Overkill," pp. 53 and 60. Until recently, however, there was little public discussion of this aspect of American strategy. For exceptions, see Arthur Lee Burns, *Ethics and Deterrence: A Nuclear Balance without Hostage Cities?* Adelphi Paper No. 69 (London: Institute for Strategic Studies, 1970); Bruce Russett, "A Countercombatant Deterrent," in Sam Sarkesian, ed., *The Military-Industrial Complex: A Reassessment* (Beverly Hills: Sage, 1972); and Russett, "Assured Destruction of What? A Countercombatant Alternative to Nuclear MADness," *Public Policy,* 22 (Spring 1974), 121–38.

11. Desmond Ball, *Targeting for Strategic Deterrence,* Adelphi Paper No. 185 (London: International Institute for Strategic Studies, 1983), p. 67.

12. The idea of seeking to destroy Communist political control also is not new. The U.S. war objectives established by NSC 5410/1, March 29, 1954, included the following: "To render ineffective the control structure by which the Soviet and Communist regimes have been able to exert ideological disciplinary authority over indivdiual citizens or groups of citizens in other countries" (quoted in Rosenberg, " 'A Smoking Radiating Ruin at the End of Two Hours,' " p. 29). Also see Rosenberg, "The Origins of Overkill," pp. 36, 57–58. Ethnic targeting seems a more recent development. See George Quester, "Ethnic Targeting: A Bad Idea Whose Time Has Come," *Journal of Strategic Studies,* 5 (June 1982), 228–35.

13. Lack of information—another possible objection to this approach—is less of an impediment to analysis than is often believed. Of course, the details of the war plans are classified, but what we care about here are the rationales for the strategy. On this point, public accounts are quite full and the plentiful leaks seem reliable.

14. James Schlesinger in U.S. Senate, Subcommittee on Arms Control, International Law and Organization of the Committee on Foreign Relations, *Hearings on U.S.–U.S.S.R. Strategic Policies,* 93d Cong., 2d sess., March 4, 1974 (Washington, D.C.: Government Printing Office, 1974), p. 8.

15. Similarly, Thomas Schelling notes that the McNamara doctrine has "occasionally been called . . . 'no-cities strategy.' As good a name would be 'cities strategy.' The newer strategy at last recognized the important of cities for. . . . [L]ive cities were to be appreciated as assets, as hostages, as a means of influence over the enemy himself": *Arms and Influence* (New Haven: Yale University Press, 1966), pp. 190–91.)

16. U.S. Senate, Committee on Foreign Relations, *Hearing on Presidential Directive 59,* 96th Cong., 2d sess., September 16, 1980 (Washington: Government Printing Office, 1981), p. 30. For a further discussion see below, pp. 110–11.

17. Glenn Snyder, *Deterrence and Defense* (Princeton: Princeton University

Press, 1961). Dennis Ross makes good use of the distinction in his analysis of Soviet doctrine in "Rethinking Soviet Strategic Policy," *Journal of Strategic Studies*, 1 (May 1978), 3–31. As Michael Howard notes, Clausewitz made a similar distinction between deterrence by "the improbability of victory" and by "its unacceptable cost": "The Issue of No First Use," Letter to the Editor, *Foreign Affairs*, 61 (Fall 1982), 211).

18. Department of Defense, *Annual Report, F.Y. 1981* (Washington, D.C.: Government Printing Office, 1980), p. 63.

19. Ibid., p. 67; DoD, *Annual Report, F.Y. 1982* (Washington, D.C.: Government Printing Office, 1981), p. 5; Haig, "Peace and Deterrence," p. 1. Examining possible Soviet gains from aggression, George Kennan makes the interesting argument that Soviets would seek to judge "not just the prospects for military victory but also the prospective availability of local Communist factions in the enemy country which could" rule in the postwar period: *The Nuclear Delusion* (New York: Pantheon, 1983), p. 130.

20. DoD, *Annual Report, F.Y. 1981*, p. 65; DoD, *Annual Report, F.Y. 1982*, p. 29 (see also DoD, *Annual Report, F.Y. 1979* [Washington, D.C.: Government Printing Office, 1978], p. 32, and DoD, *Annual Report, F.Y. 1981*, p. 66); ibid., p. 67. Emphasis added throughout.

21. Harold Brown, remarks prepared for delivery before the Council on Foreign Relations and the Foreign Policy Association, April 5, 1979; DoD, *Annual Report, F.Y. 1980* (Washington, D.C.: Government Printing Office, 1979), p. 77; DoD, *Annual Report, F.Y. 1982*, p. 39; Weinberger in U.S. Senate, Committee on Foreign Relations, *Hearings on Strategic Weapons Proposals*, part 1, 97th Cong., 1st sess. (Washington, D.C.: Government Printing Office, 1981), p. 17; also see p. 23 and Weinberger's comment in U.S. Senate, Committee on Armed Services, *Hearings on Department of Defense Authorization for Appropriations for F.Y. 1984*, part 1, 98th Cong. 1st sess. (Washington, D.C.: Government Printing Office, 1983), p. 76.

22. DoD, *Annual Report, F.Y. 1984* (Washington, D.C.: Government Printing Office, 1983), p. 34. But on page 51 of this document, both deterrence by denial and deterrence by punishment are seen as necessary.

23. Weinberger's first Defense Guidance apparently said that American nuclear forces "must prevail and be able to force the Soviet Union to seek earliest termination of hostilities on terms favorable to the United States" (quoted in Richard Halloran, "Pentagon Draws up First Strategy for Fighting a Long Nuclear War," *New York Times*, May 30, 1982). This implies a strong form of deterrence by denial, but there is no indication that the document specifies how such a goal was to be reached. A later Defense Guidance apparently abandoned this formulation ("Weinberger Drops Disputed Words in Revision of '82 Arms Proposal," *New York Times*, March 18, 1983). The current public posture is that "should deterrence fail, our strategy is to restore peace on favorable terms": DoD, *Annual Report, F.Y. 1984*, p. 34.

24. *Hearing on P.D. 59*, p. 16.

25. George Brown, *United States Military Posture for FY 1978*, (N.P., 1977), p. 6.

26. DoD, *Annual Report, F.Y. 1981*, p. 86. Also see Schlesinger's arguments in DoD, *Annual Report, F.Y. 1976* (Washington, D.C.: Government Printing Office, 1975), p. II–3; and U.S. House of Representatives, Committee on Armed Services, *Hearings on Military Posture*, part 1, February 1974, 93d Cong., 2d sess. (Washington, D.C.: Government Printing Office, 1974), p. 50.

27. *Hearing on P.D. 59*, p. 30; DoD *Annual Report, F.Y. 1979*, p. 78; Casper Weinberger, "On Nuclear War," *New York Review of Books*, August 18, 1983, p. 30; DoD, *Annual Report, F.Y. 1980*, p. 79. See also Secretary of State Haig's argument in U.S. Senate, Committee on Foreign Relations, *Hearings on Strategic Weapons Proposals*, 97th Cong., 1st sess. (Washington: Government Printing Office, 1981), p. 61, and the official statements in DoD, *Annual Report, F.Y. 1985* (Washington, D.C.: Government Printing Office, 1984), p. 27, and U.S. Senate, Committee on Appropriations, *Hearings on S. Con. Res. 26*, 98th Cong., 1st sess. (Washington, D.C.: Government Printing Office, 1983), p. 240.

28. DoD., *Annual Report, F.Y. 1980*, p. 61.

29. *Hearing on P.D. 59*, p. 3. For a further discussion of this issue, see below, pp. 153–55.

30. Colin Gray, "Targeting Problems for Central War," *Naval War College Review*, 33 (January–February 1980), 7. Also see his "Nuclear Strategy: A Case for a Theory of Victory," *International Security*, 4 (Summer 1979), pp. 54–87. The problem, it should be noted, is not with the lack of a theory of victory, but with victory's impracticality.

4. *Issues and Contradictions in the Countervailing Strategy*

1. See, for example, the discussion by Michael Howard, "Reassurance and Deterrence," *Foreign Affairs*, 61 (Winter 1982/83), 309–24.

2. See David Schwartz, *NATO's Nuclear Dilemmas* (Washington, D.C. Brookings Institution, 1983), chapter 7; Gregory Treverton, "NATO Alliance Politics," in Richard Betts, ed., *Cruise Missiles* (Washington, D.C.: Brookings Institution, 1981), pp. 415–42; Robert Art and Simon Lunn, *NATO in the Age of Strategic Parity* (forthcoming). For good general discussions of the INF issue, see McGeorge Bundy, "American in the 1980s—Reframing Our Relations with Our Friends and among Our Allies," *Survival*, 24 (January/February 1982), 24–29; Bundy "The Future of Strategic Deterrence," *Survival*, 21 (November/December 1979), 268–72; Christoper Makins, "TNF Modernization and 'Countervailing Strategy,'" *Survival*, 23 (July/August 1981), 157–64; Raymond Garthoff, "The NATO Decision on Theater Nuclear Forces," *Political Science Quarterly*, 98 (Summer 1983), 197–214; and Richard H. Ullman, "Out of the Euromissile Mire," *Foreign Policy*, No. 50 (Spring 1983), pp. 39–52.

3. Weinberger stresses "the context of the overall Soviet force buildup" in explaining why the NATO deployment is needed: Department of Defense, *Annual Report, F.Y. 1984* (Washington, D.C.: Government Printing Office, 1983), p. 56.

4. *New York Times*, November 9, 1981; DoD, *Annual Report, F.Y. 1981* (Washington, D.C.: Government Printing Office, 1980), p. 7; also see p. 147. As these

quotations imply, even before the deployment of the SS-20, the Russians could attack European targets with missiles based in the Soviet Union. See also Richard Perle's remarks in "U.S. Official Says West's Resolve Holds the European Missile Key," *San Diego Union*, February 20, 1983, and Office of the Secretary of Defense, "Modernization and Arms Control for Long-Range Theater Nuclear Forces," U.S. Rationale Paper, October 16, 1979, p. 6.

5. Michael Howard, "Case for Keeping a Strong Conventional Arms Capability," Letter to the Editor, *The Times*, (London) November 3, 1981.

6. David Holloway, *The Soviet Union and the Arms Race* (New Haven: Yale University Press, 1983), p. 69.

7. DoD, *Annual Report, F.Y. 1982* (Washington, D.C.: Government Printing Office, 1981), p. 64; Office of the Secretary of Defense, "Modernization and Arms Control," p. 11.

8. See, for example, the comments of Perle and Brown in U.S. House of Representatives, Committee on Foreign Affairs, *Overview of Nuclear Arms Control and Defense Strategy in NATO*, 97th Cong., 2d sess. (Washington, D.C.: Government Printing Office, 1982), pp. 86, 194, and the remarks of Perle in "A Debate: Does NATO Really Need Those Missiles?", *New York Times*, sec. 4, November 22, 1981.

9. Leslie Gelb, "Soviet Marshal Warns the U.S. on Its Missiles," *New York Times*, March 17, 1983. Also see Christopher Jones, "Equality and Equal Security in Europe," *Orbis* 26 (Fall 1982), p. 647; and Holloway, *The Soviet Union and the Arms Race*, p. 72. European reaction is cited by Raymond Garthoff in *Overview of Nuclear Arms Control and Defense Strategy in NATO*, pp. 115–16. Some official U.S. statements have argued that the INF deployment is exactly the right size for coupling: the proposed forces "are not so large as to imply a diminished role for strategic forces; but they are large enough to assure a militarily and politically strong link to those forces:" Office of the Secretary of Defense, "Modernization and Arms Control," p. 10. It is hard to reconcile this with the claim noted earlier that the threat to use these weapons is credible because of the "military viability" of the response.

10. Richard Burt, "NATO and Nuclear Deterrence," September 23, 1981 (U.S. Department of State, *Current Policy*, No. 319), pp. 2–3; Henry Kissinger, "Nuclear Weapons and the Peace Movement," *Washington Quarterly*, 5 (Summer 1982), 34; "Statement by Reagan on War," *New York Times*, October 22, 1981. Also see Richard Perle's statements in "A Debate: Does NATO Really Need Those Missiles?" It is hard to square this view of coupling with Kissinger's argument that Brezhnev's statements "to the effect that if one nuclear weapon is used, then 'unavoidably' the conflict will assume a 'global' character" is a "threatening" one. ("Something Is Deeply Wrong in the Atlantic Alliance," *Washington Post*, December 21, 1981.) Why should the same posture be defensive when held by United States and aggressive when taken by the Soviet Union?

11. Howard, "Case for Keeping a Strong Conventional Arms Capability." Analysis of a number of cases indicates that deterrence is most likely to succeed when there are close ties between the states making the deterrence threat and the country it is seeking to protect. See Bruce Russett, "The Calculus of

Deterrence," *Journal of Conflict Resolution*, 7 (June 1983), 97–109, and Paul Huth and Bruce Russett, "What Makes Deterrence Work? Cases from 1900 to 1980," *World Politics* (forthcoming, 1984).

12. The Soviets might, on the other hand, be able to attack NATO tactical nuclear forces with nonnuclear bombs or command forces. If what causes escalation is not the damage done, but the kind of weapons used, such a move would be less likely to trigger the American strategic force.

13. Kissinger, "Nuclear Weapons and the Peace Movement," p. 34; see also Kissinger, "Arms Control and Europe's Nuclear Shield," *Wall Street Journal*, January 31, 1984. It should be noted that being in this dilemma would also give the Soviets added incentives for a preemptive strike. See Ullman, "Out of the Euromissile Mire," pp. 46–47.

14. This is further evidence of the point discussed above that the Soviets do not think in terms of limited nuclear war. If they planned to use or threaten tactical nuclear warfare to conquer Europe, they would do all they could to increase the chances that such a war would be restricted to the Continent. This would call for basing all their nuclear weapons outside of the Soviet homeland. Marshal Nikolai Ogarkov's recent statement that the use of tactical nuclear weapons would set off a world war also points to this conclusion. See above, pp. 90–91.

15. For acknowledgments of this problem, see Richard Perle in U.S. Senate, Committee on Armed Services, *Hearings on Department of Defense Authorization for Appropriations for Fiscal Year 1983*, part 7, 97th Cong., 2d sess. (Washington: D.C.: Government Printing Office, 1982), and Eugene Rostow in "Arms Control—After the Shock," *Baltimore Sun*, February 22, 1983.

16. Bernard Brodie, *Escalation and the Nuclear Option* (Princeton: Princeton University Press, 1966).

17. One of Brown's attempts to provide reassurance on this point was unfortunate: "The United States is committed to the integrity and security of Western Europe because it is in the vital interest of the United States to defend Europe. We followed that course in 1917 and again in 1941" (DoD, *Annual Report, F.Y. 1981*, p. 96). This overlooks the fact that the United States entered World War I only after Germany lifted all restrictions against attacking American shipping, and World War II only after the American homeland was attacked.

18. Kissinger, "Nuclear weapons and the Peace Movement," p. 34. Note that this would apply to current TNF as well as to INF.

19. DoD, *Annual Report, F.Y. 1984*, p. 56. Weinberger prefaces his statement by mentioning "NATO's ability to retaliate against the Soviet Union from Europe," but it is not clear why this capability is necessary for the Russians to fear that the war would not remain limited.

20. DoD, *Annual Report, F.Y. 1982*, p. 64.

21. The figure comes from Jeffrey Richelson, "P.D.-59, NSDD-13 and the Reagan Strategic Modernization Program," *Journal of Strategic Studies*, 6 (June 1983), 131–36. This assumes using two warheads for each target. Similar figures can be found in William Beecher, "U.S. Drafts New N-War Strategy vs. Soviets," *Boston Globe*, July 27, 1980, and Desmond Ball, "Issues in Strategic

Nuclear Targeting: Target Selection and Rates of Fire," paper delivered at the Annual Meeting of the American Political Science Association, September 1982, pp. 7–8. Not all the leadership shelters have C^3 facilities, however, and those lacking them might not be high-priority targets. Data on the number of targets in various categories can be found in Desmond Ball, *Targeting for Strategic Deterrence*, Adelphi Paper No. 185 (London: International Institute for Strategic Studies, 1983) and Barry Posen and Stephen Van Evera, "Defense Policy and the Reagan Administration," *International Security*, 8 (Summer 1983), 13–14. Again, the problem is not new. The targets the Air Force seeks to destroy are always more numerous than the warheads available. See, for example, the 1959 position discussed by David Rosenberg, "The Origins of Overkill: Nuclear Weapons and American Strategy, 1945–1960," *International Security*, 7 (Spring 1983), 58.

22. The ability of Minuteman III with its Mark 12A warhead to destroy hardened Soviet targets is in dispute. See the exchanges in U.S. Senate, Committee on Appropriations, *Hearings on S. Con. Res. 26*, 98th Cong., 1st sess. (Washington, D.C.: Government Printing Office, 1983), pp. 200, 205, 211.

23. Desmond Ball, *Can the Nuclear War Be Controlled?* Adelphi Paper No. 169 (London: International Institute for Strategic Studies, Autumn 1981), p. 21.

24. Ibid.; Congressional Budget Office, *Strategic Command, Control, and Communications: Alternative Approaches for Modernization* (Washington, D.C.: Congress of the United States, 1981); Frank Klotz, "The U.S. President and the Control of Strategic Nuclear Weapons (Ph.D. diss., Oxford University, 1980): John Steinbruner, "Launch under Attack," *Scientific American*, 250 (January 1984), 37–47.

25. Some of these problems disappear if the brigadier general who commands the Strategic Air Command's flying command post has the authority to fire the nuclear weapons if Washington is destroyed. Only a few officials know whether this delegation of authority is planned.

26. Strobe Talbott, *Endgame*, (New York: Harper & Row, 1979), p. 171.

27. Walter Slocombe claims the capabilities are now in place, but gives no evidence:"The Countervailing Strategy,"*International Security*, 5 (Spring 1981), 27.

28. Wallace Thies, *When Governments Collide* (Berkeley: University of California Press, 1980).

29. Thus when David Jones retired as chairman of the Joint Chiefs of Staff he declared: "If you try to do everything to fight a protracted nuclear war, then you end up with the potential of a bottomless pit" (quoted in Richard Halloran, "Top General Questions Policy on Prolonged A-War," *New York Times*, June 19, 1982). In 1979, the head of SAC apparently told Secretary Brown that current U.S. strategic forces could not implement the proposed P.D.-59 (Drew Middleton, "SAC Chief Is Critical of Carter's New Nuclear Plan," *New York Times*, September 7, 1980). The lack of practicality was one of the grounds on which the Air Force opposed McNamara's strategy; see Rosenberg, "The Origins of Overkill," p. 70, and Desmond Ball, *Politics and Force Levels: The Strategic Missile Program of the Kennedy Administration* (Berkeley: University of California Press, 1980).

30. For an example of the first claim, see Schlesinger's remarks in U.S.

House of Representatives, *Hearings on Military Posture,* part 1, February 1974, 93rd Cong., 2d sess. (Washington, D.C.: Government Printing Office, 1974), p. 29; and Kissinger's "NATO Defense and the Soviet Threat," *Survival,* 21 (November/December 1979), 267 (although the thrust of his arguments undercuts this position). For an example of the second claim, see DoD, *Annual Report, F.Y. 1981,* p. 88. One of the studies done in the early days of the Nixon administration which called for limited nuclear options admitted that such attacks "have no precedent in Soviet military doctrine or tradition" (quoted in Fred Kaplan, *The Wizards of Armageddon* [New York: Simon & Schuster, 1983], p. 366).

31. Lynn Davis, *Limited Nuclear Options,* Adelphi Paper No. 121 (London: International Institute for Strategic Studies, Winter 1975–76), p. 7.

32. "Evaluation of Effect on Soviet War Effort Resulting from the Strategic Air Offensive," May 11, 1949, in Thomas Etzold and John Gaddis, eds., *Containment: Documents on American Policy and Strategy, 1945–1950* (New York: Columbia University Press, 1978), p. 362.

33 DoD, *Annual Report, F.Y. 1982,* p. 38.

34. Benjamin Lambeth and Kevin Lewis, "Economic Targeting in Nuclear War," *Orbis* 27 (Spring 1983), p. 144. John Erickson, "The Soviet View of Deterrence: A General Survey," *Survival,* 24 (November/December 1982), 246.

The literature on Soviet doctrine is enormous. Excellent treatment can be found in Robert Arnett, "Soviet Attitudes toward Nuclear War: Do They Really Think They Can Win?" *Journal of Strategic Studies,* 2 (September 1979), 172–92; Holloway, *The Soviet Union and the Arms Race,* pp. 29–64; Jack Snyder, *The Soviet Strategic Culture: Implications for Limited Nuclear Operations* (Santa Monica, Calif.: RAND Corp., R-2034-DDRE, December 1976); James McConnell, *Soviet and American Strategic Doctrines: One More Time* (Alexandria, Va.: Center for Naval Analyses, January 1980), Professional Paper 271.

35. U.S. Senate, Committee on Foreign Relations, *Hearing on Presidential Directive 59,* 96th Cong., 2d sess., September 16, 1980 (Washington, D.C.: Government Printing Office, 1981), p. 8. This was Schlesinger's position also. See U.S. Senate, Subcommittee on Foreign Relations, *Briefing on Counterforce Attacks,* 93d Cong., 2d sess. (Washington, D.C.: Government Printing Office, 1975), p. 9, and DoD, *Annual Report, F.Y. 1975* (Washington, D.C.: Government Printing Office, 1974), p. 4.

36. Nathan Leites, *A Study of Bolshevism* (Glencoe, Ill.: Free Press, 1953); Snyder, *The Soviet Strategic Culture.*

37. Holloway, *The Soviet Union and the Arms Race,* p. 43; DoD, *Annual Report, F.Y. 1982,* p. 38.

38. Richard Pipes reaches the same conclusion: "The Russians certainly accept the *fact* of deterrence" even though "they regard it as undesirable and transient": "Why the Russians Think They Could Fight and Win a Nuclear War," *Commentary,* July 1977, p. 29.

39. U.S. Senate, Subcommittee on Arms Control, International Law and Organization of the Committee on Foreign Relations, *Hearing on U.S. and Soviet Strategic Doctrine and Military Policies,* 93d Cong., 2d sess., March 4, 1974 (Washington, D.C.: Government Printing Office, 1974), p. 13.

40. DoD, *Annual Report, F.Y. 1981*, p. 67 (the sentences expressing greatest doubt were apparently writen by Brown himself: see Kaplan, *Wizards of Armageddon*, pp. 385–86). Secretary of State Haig took the same position. See "Peace and Deterrence," April 6, 1982 (U.S. Department of State, *Current Policy*, No. 383), p. 2.

41. Colin Gray, "Defense, War Fighting, and Deterrence," *Naval War College Review*, 35 (July–August 1982), 41. Also see Schlesinger's position in *Briefing on Counterforce Attacks*, pp. 37–38.

42. *Hearing on P.D. 59*, p. 30.

43. DoD, *Annual Report, F.Y. 1981*, p. 66.

44. *Report of the President's Commission on Strategic Forces* (hereafter *Scowcroft Report*), April 6, 1983, p. 6. Also see Henry Kissinger, "NATO: The Next Thirty Years," *Survival*, 21 (November/December 1979), 267.

45. Morgan Strong's interview with Edward Rowny, "We Must Overcome Soviet Missile Edge," *USA Today*, August 31, 1983; Brad Knickerbocker, "How MX Missile Fits into Shifting Arms Strategy," *Christian Science Monitor*, May 5, 1983. For a statement that matches U.S. warheads with Soviet targets, see *Hearings on S. Con. Res. 26.*, p. 259.

46. *Scowcroft Report*, p. 8.

47. Ibid, pp. 12, 14, and 16–17. Also see *Hearings on S. Con. Res. 26*, pp. 92–3, 122.

48. See the discussion above, pp. 44–45, and below, pp. 123–24.

49. *Scowcroft Report*, p. 18.

50. U.S. House of Representatives, Committee on Armed Services, *Hearings on H.R. 2287, Department of Defense Authorization of Appropriations for F.Y. 1984*, 98th Cong., 1st sess. (Washington, D.C.: Government Printing Office, 1983), p. 116. Also see *Hearings on S. Con. Res. 26*, pp. 167–68, 258, 260.

51. George Shultz, "Modernizing U.S. Strategic Forces," April 20, 1983, (U.S. Department of State, *Current Policy*, No. 480), p. 2. One should note that while Shultz bases some of his position on Soviet perceptions, there is no evidence that the Russians in fact see the world as he thinks they do; they do not seem to attribute special properties to U.S. ICBMs.

52. Richard Halloran, "Pentagon Draws Up First Strategy for Fighting a Long Nuclear War," *New York Times*, May 30, 1982.

53. DoD, *Annual Report, F.Y. 1982*, pp. 41–42. Again, the problem is not a new one; it has plagued U.S. war planning from the start. See the discussion in Gregg Herken, *The Winning Weapon* (New York: Knopf, 1980), pp. 268–80.

54. Herken, *The Winning Weapon*, p. 317. This was stated as official U.S. policy in April 1973 by Secretary of Defense Elliot Richardson in U.S. House of Representatives, Committee on Armed Services, *Hearings on Military Posture and H.R. 6722*, 93rd Cong., 1st sess. (Washington, D.C.: Government Printing Office, 1973), pp. 498–99. It should also be noted that keeping Soviet casualties down in a counterforce war would be difficult because of the co-location of Russian missile fields and population centers. See Desmond Ball, "Research Note: Soviet ICBM Deployment," *Survival*, 22 (July/August 1980), 167–70.

55. Richard Perle, in United States Senate, Subcommittee on Arms Control,

Oceans, International Operations, and Environment of the Committee on Foreign Relations, *Hearings on United States and Soviet Civil Defense Programs*, 97th Cong., 2d sess. (Washington: Government Printing Office, 1972), p. 48.

56. Quoted in Ball, *Can Nuclear War Be Controlled?*, p. 29. Public attention to this question began with discussion of the Schlesinger doctrine. See *Briefings on Counterforce Attacks*; U.S. Senate, Subcommittee on Arms Control, International Organizations and Security Agreements of the Committe on Foreign Relations, *Analyses of Effects of Limited Nuclear Warfare*, 94th Cong., 1st sess. (Washington, D.C.: Government Printing Office, 1975).

57. George Quester, *Nuclear Diplomacy* (New York: Dunellen, 1970), p. 246.

58. Drew Middleton, "U.S. Rearmed: Will Strategy Alter Soviet's?" *New York Times*, November 2, 1981.

59. DoD, *Annual Report, F.Y. 1980* (Washington, D.C.: Government Printing Office, 1979), p. 78.

60. U.S. House of Representatives, Committee on the Budget, *Economic Outlook for the Second Budget Resolution*, 97th Cong., 1st sess. (Washington, D.C.: Government Printing Offices, 1981), p. 242.

61. Consistent with this is the recent statement by James Watkins, Chief of Naval Operations, that the United States should improve its capability to destroy Soviet submarines hiding under the Arctic ice ("Admiral Urges U.S. to Counter Under-Ice Subs," *International Herald Tribune*, May 20, 1983).

62. Quoted in Richard Halloran, "Weinberger Defends His Plan to Fight Long Nuclear War," *New York Times*, August 10, 1982. Weinberger is quoted in the same article as saying, "You show me a Secretary of Defense who's planning not to prevail and I'll show you a Secretary of Defense who ought to be impeached." Also see his statement in DoD, *Annual Report, F.Y. 1983* (Washington, D.C.: Government Printing Office, 1982), p. I-18. But it is not clear whether this is more than a shift in rhetoric which, furthermore, has been at least partially reversed (see "Weinberger Drops Disputed Words in Revision of '82 Arms Proposal," *New York Times*, March 18, 1983). Some people argue that Reagan's policy, unlike Carter's, holds that mutual security is impossible and seeks to make the Russians insecure in order to coerce them and reduce their influence. Although the statments of some White House officials support this view, I believe it is exaggerated.

63. A similar contradiction should be noted on the other end of the political spectrum. Most of those who argue that the United States does not have to be concerned about the vulnerability of its ICBMs also argue that the MX would be dangerous because it could destroy Soviet missiles. Of course the Russians have a larger proportion of their forces based on land, but nevertheless worrying more about the vulnerability of Soviet ICBMs than American ones may be carrying internationalism a bit too far.

64. Jervis, "Cooperation under the Security Dilemma," *World Politics*, 30 (January 1978), 186–214.

65. Paul Nitze, "Policy and Strategy from Weakness," in W. Scott Thompson, ed., *National Security in the 1980s: From Weakness to Strength* (San Francisco: Institute for Contemporary Studies, 1980); Brown, DoD, *Annual Report, F.Y.*

1981, p. 68. While this statement might be dismissed as self-serving, the same explanation cannot be easily applied to the statements I have quoted in the next paragraph.

66. Quoted in Richard Halloran, "Brown Warns that a Persian Gulf War Could Spread," *New York Times*, February 15, 1980; quoted in Charles Caudry, "Brown Says Moscow Risks All-Out War if It Decides to March on Persian Gulf," *Baltimore Sun*, January 12, 1981. Also see DoD, *Annual Report, F.Y. 1981*, p. 67. Similarly, in the Cuban missile crisis the United States dispersed bombers to civilian air fields, and Kennedy announced: "It shall be the policy of this nation to regard any nuclear missile launched from Cuba against any nation in the Western Hemisphere as an attack by the Soviet Union on the United States, requiring a full retaliatory response upon the Soviet Union." As George Quester notes, this was contrary to the McNamara doctrine (*Nuclear Diplomacy*, p. 246). "Excerpts from interview with President Reagan conducted by five reporters," *New York Times*, February 3, 1981. Also see Kenneth Waltz, "A Strategy for the Rapid Deployment Force," *International Security*, 5 (Spring 1981), 49–73, and the discussion in Chapter 6 below.

5. *Escalation Dominance and Competition in Risk-Taking*

1. Quoted in Amoretta Hoeber and Francis Hoeber, "The Case against the Case against Counterforce," *Strategic Review*, 3 (Fall 1975), 63.

2. Colin Gray, "Targeting Problems for Central War," *Naval War College Review*, 33 (January–February 1980), 15. See also Benjamin Lambeth and Kevin Lewis, "Economic Targeting in Nuclear War: U.S. and Soviet Approaches," *Orbis*, 27 (Spring 1983), 147–49.

3. Department of Defense, *Annual Report, F.Y. 1979* (Washington, D.C.: Government Printing Office, 1978), p. 56; DoD, *Annual Report, F.Y. 1982* (Washington, D.C.: Government Printing Office, 1981), p. 58. When he first took office, Brown made a much stronger claim: "Only if our defenses are appropriate and adequate to meet the main contingencies can our posture of deterrence be considered credible": U.S. House of Representatives, Committee on Armed Services, *Hearings on Military Posture and H.R. 5068*, 95th Cong., 1st sess. (Washington, D.C.: Government Printing Office, 1977), p. 97.

4. For a discussion of the dangers which would follow from the belief that war was inevitable, see pp. 165–67. I am assuming that C^3 facilities are invulnerable. In fact, this is not likely to be the case, and attacking them may give the attacker a slight but significant chance of escaping unscathed.

5. Thomas Schelling, *Arms and Influence* (New Haven: Yale University Press, 1966), pp. 166–68. The discussion in this section is greatly influenced by James King, "The New Strategy" (unpublished MS). The distinction between escalation dominance and competition in risk-taking has some parallel in John Gaddis's distinction between symmetrical and asymmetrical strategies of containment: *Strategies of Containment* (New York: Oxford University Press, 1982).

6. DoD, *Annual Report, F.Y. 1984* (Washington, D.C.: Government Printing Office, 1983), p. 51; also see p. 57.

7. Sam Nunn, "NATO: Saving the Alliance," *Washington Quarterly*, 5 (Summer 1982), p. 21.

8. U.S. Senate, Committee on Armed Services, *Hearings on the Military Implications of the SALT II Treaty*, part 3, 96th Cong., 1st sess. (Washington, D.C.: Government Printing Office, 1979), pp. 888–89.

9. Michael Howard, "The Issue of No First Use," Letter to the Editor, *Foreign Affairs*, 61 (Fall 1982), 212. Emphasis omitted.

10. I think this subject needs more discussion. For treatments of it see Thomas Schelling, *Arms and Influence*, pp. 78–86; Robert Jervis, "Deterrence Theory Revisited," *World Politics*, 31 (January 1979), 317–18. Also below, pp. 153–57. The question is complicated by the fact that the distinction between deterrence and compellence is not always clear. For a discussion of the Cuban missile crisis which brings this out well, see Raymond Garthoff, "Soviet Perceptions of Western Strategic Thought and Doctrine," in *Soviet Military Doctrine and Western Security Policy* (Paris: Atlantic Institute for International Affairs, forthcoming).

11. Schelling, *Arms and Influence*, pp. 104, 106; also see p. 109.

12. Warner Schilling, "U.S. Strategic Nuclear Concept in the 1970s: The Search for Sufficient Equivalent Countervailing Parity," *International Security*, 6 (Fall 1981), 72.

13. Richard Ned Lebow, "Misconceptions in American Strategic Assessment," *Political Science Quarterly*, 97 (Summer 1982), 196; also see Jervis, "Why Nuclear Superiority Doesn't Matter,' *Political Science Quarterly*, 94 (Winter 1979–80), 617–34; Bernard Brodie, *War and Politics* (New York: Macmillan, 1973), pp. 363–64; and Patrick Morgan, *Deterrence* (Beverly Hills, Calif.: Sage, 1977), pp. 136–43.

14. Brodie, *War and Politics*, p. 412. Emphasis deleted. President Eisenhower similarly thought it was " 'fatuous' to think that a conflict between the United States and the U.S.S.R. could take place without atomic weapons being employed": Douglas Kinnard, *President Eisenhower and Strategy Management* (Lexington, Ky.: University Press of Kentucky, 1977), p. 55. Other analysts who share Brodie's general views disagree on this point, stressing the importance of local conventional superiority as a determinant of the outcome of the missile crisis. See, for example, McGeorge Bundy, "The Bishops and the Bomb," *New York Review of Books*, June 16, 1983, p. 4.

15. Brodie, *War and Politics*, pp. 415–16.

16. Alexander George, David Hall, and William Simons, *The Limits of Coercive Diplomacy* (Boston: Little, Brown, 1971), p. 113. As George notes, Kennedy also felt these pressures keenly and indeed "wavered at the last minute and was inclined to avoid the confrontation with the Soviet submarine" near the blockade (pp. 113–14). This demonstration can also be considered an example of the threat that leaves something to chance, as discussed below. For general discussions of the importance of resolve, see Stephen Maxwell, *Rationality in Deterrence*, Adelphi Paper No. 50 (London: Institute for Strategic Studies, 1968); Alexander George and Richard Smoke, *Deterrence in American Foreign*

Policy (New York: Columbia University Press, 1974); Steven Rosen, "A Model of War and Alliance," in Julian Freedman, Christopher Bladen, and Steven Rosen, *Alliance in International Politics* (Boston: Allyn & Bacon, 1970), pp. 215–37; Rosen, "War Power and Willingness to Suffer," in Bruce Russett, ed., *Peace, War, and Numbers* (Beverly Hills, Calif.: Sage, 1972), pp. 167–83; Glenn Snyder, " 'Prisoner's Dilemma' and 'Chicken' Models in International Policies," *International Studies Quarterly*, 15 (March 1971), 66–103; Robert Jervis, "Deterrence Theory Revisited," pp. 314–22; and Zeev Maoz, "Resolve, Capabilities, and the Outcomes of Interstate Disputes," *Journal of Conflict Resolution*, 27 (June 1983), 195–230. For a somewhat different view, see Harrison Wagner, "Deterrence and Bargaining," *Journal of Conflict Resolution*, 26 (June 1982), 329–58. For a discussion of the role of limited nuclear strikes in this process, see the essays in Klaus Knorr and Thornton Read, *Limited Strategic War* (New York: Praeger, 1962).

17. Bernard Brodie, "What Price Conventional Capabilities in Europe?", *The Reporter*, May 23, 1963, p. 32.

18. Schelling, *Arms and Influence*, pp. 98–99. Schelling provides no supporting arguments for the claim that military superiority provides any assistance in this process and, in an era of nuclear plenty, I do not think the claim is correct. Indeed, a little later Schelling notes that "If the clash of a squad with a division can lead to unintended war . . . , their potencies are equal in respect of the threats that count" (p. 103). Stephen Peter Rosen argues that military advantage was vital to determining each side's resolve in Vietnam, but this was a long and costly struggle for what was to the United States a relatively minor objective. Furthermore, after U.S. involvement reached a high level, the fear of escalation could exert pressure only on the U.S., and even here it was not the major consideration. See Rosen, "Vietnam and the American Theory of Limited War," *International Security*, 7 (Fall 1982), 83–113.

19. Thomas Schelling, *The Strategy of Conflict* (Cambridge: Harvard University Press, 1960), pp. 187–204. For an excellent discussion of alternative meanings of this concept, see Robert Powell, "The Theoretical Foundations of Strategic Nuclear Deterrence," (unpublished MS, Department of Economics, University of California at Berkeley).

20. Morton Halperin, *Limited War in the Nuclear Age* (New York: Wiley, 1963).

21. Samuel Huntington, "The Renewal of Strategy," in Huntington, ed., *The Strategic Imperative: New Policies for American Security* (Cambridge: Ballinger, 1982), p. 13; also see p. 33. Kissinger's view is similar, if more dramatically put: "I have sat around the NATO Council table . . . and have uttered the magic words [reassuring NATO of the American nuclear committment]. . . . and yet if my analysis is correct these words cannot be true, and . . . we must face the fact that it is absurd to base the strategy of the West on the credibility of the threat of mutual suicide": "NATO: The Next Thirty Years," *Survival*, 21 (November/December 1979), 266. Although disputing most of Kissinger's ideas on strategy, McNamara agrees on this point. See his "The Military Role of Nuclear Weapons," *Foreign Affairs*, 62 (Fall 1983), pp. 67–68, 73.

22. Bromley Smith, "Summary Record of NSC Executive Committee Meet-

ing No. 5, October 25, 1962, 5:00 PM," John F. Kennedy Library, Boston, p. 3. In retrospect, this judgment seems bizarre. But in many areas the relative riskiness of various actions is still hard to determine. For example, Brodie argues: "I see no basis in experience or logic for assuming that the increase in level of violence from one division to thirty [in a conventional war in Europe] is a less shocking and less dangerous form of escalation than the introduction of [tactical] nuclear weapons": "What Price Conventional Capabilities in Europe?", p. 32.) Most analysts would disagree (and so would I), but in reaching our conclusions we must all rely heavily on intuition.

23. For examples of types of unintentional escalation, see Richard Smoke, *War: Controlling Escalation* (Cambridge: Harvard University Press, 1977).

24. John Harvey, ed., *The Diplomatic Diaries of Oliver Harvey* (New York: St. Martin, 1970), p. 110, also see pp. 122–32; Imanuel Geiss, ed., *July 1914* (New York: Scribner, 1967), p. 211, also pp. 205, 289. For similar arguments in another context, see Henry Kissinger, *White House Years* (Boston: Little, Brown, 1979), p. 926.

25. DoD, *Annual Report, F.Y. 1984* (Washington, D.C.: Government Printing Office, 1983), p. 56.

26. Brodie, "AFAG Talk: Political Impact of U.S. Force Postures," May 28, 1963, p. 7, in *Fourteen Informal Writings from The Unpublished Work of Bernard Brodie, 1952–1965* (Santa Monica, Calif.: RAND Corporation). Also see Schelling, *Arms and Influence*, p. 96.

27. Henry Kissinger made this point in *Nuclear Weapons and Foreign Policy* (New York: Harper, 1957), pp. 144, 188–89, although his later views have been very different.

28. Quoted in Christopher Paine, "The Illusive 'Margin of Safety,'" *Bulletin of the Atomic Scientists*, 38 (May 1982), 13.

29. Fred Iklé, "Arms Control and National Defense," in Peter Duignan and Alvin Rabushka, eds., *The United States in the 1980s* (Stanford: Hoover Institution Press, 1980), p. 432.

30. Walter Slocombe, "The Countervailing Strategy," *International Security*, 5 (Spring 1981), 24–25; also see above, pp. 107–9.

31. DoD, *Annual Report, F.Y. 1982* (Washington, D.C.: Government Printing Office, 1981), p. 42.

32. Brodie, "What Price Conventional Capabilities in Europe?", p. 32.

33. Glenn Snyder and Paul Diesing, *Conflict among Nations* (Princeton: Princeton University Press, 1977), p. 242.

34. Of course when one state feels much more strongly than another the former can prevail, even in compellence, although it is militarily inferior at all levels. Thus Iceland was able to win the Cod War against England. In many cases, a strong ally will make concessions to a weaker one because the costs are less for it than for its partner and both sides would suffer greatly if relations badly deteriorated.

35. Of course Japan's military failure would have lowered the costs for Britain and the United States because they could have stayed on the defensive. Still, these costs would not have been small, especially if the Allies felt that a satisfactory outcome required them to conquer Japan.

36. For a discussion of this case, see Janice Stein, "Calculation, Miscalcula-tion, and Conventional Deterrence," in Robert Jervis, Richard Ned Lebow, and Janice Stein, eds., *Psychology and Deterrence* (forthcoming).

37. Benjamin Lambeth, "Uncertainties for the Soviet War Planner," *International Security*, 7 (Winter 1982/83), 139–66; also see Allen Lynch, "The Soviet Study of International Relations, 1968–1982" (Ph.D. diss., Columbia University, 1984), pp. 310–26.

38. *Department of State Bulletin*, 69 (November 19, 1973), 645.

39. *Department of State Bulletin*, 14 (November 12, 1962), 741; "The Present International Situation and the Foreign Policy of the Soviet Union," *Current Digest of the Soviet Press*, 14 (January 16, 1963), 7.

40. Nathan Leites, *A Study of Bolshevism* (Glencoe, Ill.: Free Press, 1953); George and Smoke, *Deterrence in American Foreign Policy*, pp. 527–30.

6. Conclusions

1. Department of Defense, *Annual Report, F.Y. 1980* (Washington, D.C.: Government Printing Office, 1979), p. 75. Colin Gray makes a similar error when he argues that if the United States had a large counterforce advantage over the Soviet Union, it could threaten to attack Soviet strategic forces in response to a Russian invasion of Western Europe, "secure in the knowledge that the United States had a residual ICBM force that could deter attack upon itself": "The Strategic Forces Triad: End of the Road?", *Foreign Affairs*, 56 (July 1978), 788.

2. Bernard Brodie, *Escalation and the Nuclear Option* (Princeton: Princeton University Press, 1966).

3. Barry Posen, "Inadvertant Nuclear War? Escalation and NATO's North-ern Flank," *International Security*, 7 (Fall 1982), 28–54.

4. Robert McNamara, "The Military Role of Nuclear Weapons," *Foreign Affairs*, 62, (Fall 1983), 68.

5. DoD, *Annual Report, F.Y. 1980*, p. 76. Also see Bernard Brodie, *War and Politics* (New York: Macmillan, 1973), pp. 409–11, and Fred Iklé, "Arms Control and National Defense," in Peter Duignan and Alvin Rabushka, eds., *The United States in the 1980s* (Stanford: Hoover Institution Press, 1980), pp. 427–28.

6. One can argue that the conventional balance will strongly influence the outcome because the line of battle will be an obvious possibility for a postwar settlement. But no one thinks the Russians would go to war to move the border a few miles west.

7. Glenn Snyder, "'Prisoner's Dilemma' and 'Chicken' Models in International Politics," *International Studies Quarterly*, 15 (March 1971), 82–103. This is not to claim that Chicken is an entirely appropriate model for all aspects of a superpower crisis. If military forces were alerted or mobilized on a large scale, the interactions between the two sides would be extremely complex and leaders would have incomplete and inaccurate information not only about what the other side was doing, but also about the actions of their own forces. (I am grateful to John Steinbruner for discussion on this point.)

8. Thomas Schelling, *Arms and Influence* (New York: Yale University Press, 1966), pp. 69–90; David Baldwin, "Thinking About Threats," *Journal of Conflict Resolution,* 15, (March 1971), 71–78; Baldwin, "Inter-Nation Influence Revisited," *Journal of Conflict Resolution,* 15 (December 1971), 471–86; Robert Jervis, "Deterrence Theory Revisited," *World Politics,* 31 (January 1979), 317–18; Kenneth Waltz, *The Spread of Nuclear Weapons: More May Be Better,* Adelphi Paper No. 171 (London: International Institute for Strategic Studies, 1981); Alexander George, *Managing U.S.–Soviet Rivalry* (Boulder, Colo.: Westview, 1983), pp. 381–93.

9. To some extent, this is the product of bipolarity. For a discussion, see Kenneth Waltz, "The Stability of a Bipolar World," *Daedalus,* 93 (Summer 1964), 881–909. Also see Waltz, *Theory of International Politics* (Reading, Mass.: Addison-Wesley, 1979), pp. 161–93.

10. See Jervis, "Deterrence Theory Revisited," pp. 303–4, and the literature cited there. In rebuttal, one could point to President Kennedy's belief that the chance of war in the Cuban missile crisis was between one-third and one-half: see Theodore Sorensen, *Kennedy* (New York: Harper & Row, 1965), p. 705. Running this kind of risk does not seem consistent with the argument I am making here. In reply, I would note that Kennedy thought the risk of war was even greater if he did not take a firm stand; see Jack Snyder, "Rationality at the Brink," *World Politics,* 30 (April 1978), 345–65. Furthermore, it is not at all clear that this report should be taken at face value rather than as an after-the-fact exaggeration.

11. Patrick Morgan, *Deterrence* (Beverly Hills, Calif.: Sage, 1977).

12. McGeorge Bundy, "The Bishops and the Bomb," *New York Review of Books,* June 16, 1983, pp. 3–8.

13. This condition is discussed below, pp. 165–67.

14. Of course this is one of the basic themes of Brodie's writings. See especially *War and Politics* (New York: Macmillan, 1973), chapter 1. In the same vein, in responding to those who claim that the countervailing strategy fits with Clausewitz's admonition to keep military policy in line with foreign policy, Michael Howard argues that because it neglects this question "the bulk of American thinking [has] been exactly what Clausewitz described—something that, because it is divorced from any political context, is 'pointless and devoid of sense'": "On Fighting a Nuclear War," *International Security,* 5 (Spring 1981), 9.

15. Scowcroft is thus quoted in Steven Roberts, "Politics Is Cited as Key Factor in MX Decision," *New York Times,* April 19, 1983 (also see Scowcroft's statement in U.S. House of Representatives, Committee on Armed Services, *Hearings on H.R. 2287, Department of Defense Authorization of Appropriations for F.Y. 1984,* 98th Cong. 1st sess. [Washington, D.C.: Government Printing Office 1983], p. 63, and the remarks by Brown and Brzezinski in Robert Toth, "President Stirs Broad Debate on Arms Superiority," *Los Angeles Times,* March 27, 1983); "The Left's Victory," *Wall Street Journal,* August 1, 1983. For a general discussion of how perception of resolve is determined see Robert Jervis, "Deterrence and Perception," *International Security,* (Winter 1982/83), 3–14, and Jervis, "Information Processing, Decision-Making, and Deterrence," in

Jervis, Richard Ned Lebow, and Janice Stein, eds., *Psychology and Deterrence*, forthcoming. For a historical example, see David Kaiser, "Germany and the Origins of the First World War," *Journal of Modern History*, 55 (September 1983), 447.

16. George Kennan, "On Nuclear War," *New York Review of Books*, January 21, 1982, p. 10.

17. Brodie, "On the Objectives of Arms Control," *International Security*, 1 (Summer 1976), 17–36. Indeed, if one argues that the strategic balance is stable, it is hard to argue logically that a dangerous arms race exists and needs to to be curbed by arms-control agreements. If neither side needs to worry that the other may gain a nuclear superiority, why are treaties needed? (This point is not missed by proponents of the countervailing strategy: see, for example, Schlesinger in DoD, *Annual Report, F.Y. 1975* [Washington, D.C.: Government Printing Office, 1974], p. 39.) One possible argument is that domestic politics would not permit limiting American programs without such agreements.

18. Alexander George and Richard Smoke, *Deterrence in American Foreign Policy* (New York: Columbia University Press, 1974).

19. For a further discussion of this kind of consistency, see Robert Jervis, *Perception and Misperception in International Politics* (Princeton: Princeton University Press, 1976), pp. 128–43, and Jervis, "Beliefs about Soviet Behavior," comment in Robert Osgood, *Containment, Soviet Behavior, and Grand Strategy* (University of California at Berkeley: Institute of International Studies, 1981), pp. 55–59. For studies of past events which try to get at this question, see Barry Blechman and Stephen Kaplan, *Force without War: U.S. Armed Forces as a Political Instrument* (Washington, D.C.: Brookings Institution, 1978); Richard Betts, "Elusive Equivalence: The Political and Military Meaning of the Nuclear Balance," in Samuel Huntington, ed., *The Strategic Imperative: New Policies for American Security* (Cambridge: Ballinger, 1982), pp. 111–17; and Klaus Knorr, *On the Uses of Military Power in the Nuclear Age* (Princeton: Princeton University Press, 1966).

20. Some opponents of the countervailing strategy oppose the development of limited nuclear options on the grounds that American leaders might be tempted to use them in a situation where in their absence the United States would be restrained. Although these fears cannot be entirely dismissed, I think they are exaggerated. Furthermore, they do not easily fit with the view that such options are unnecessary because the Soviets are easy to deter. Why should American leaders be seen as more reckless than Soviet ones?

21. George Kennan, "Zero Options," *New York Review of Books*, May 12, 1983, p. 3. Kennan's position on this question has not changed. According to his memoirs, in the late 1940s: "Time and again . . . I said to my colleagues: All right, the Russians are well armed and we are poorly armed So what: We are like a man who has let himself into a walled garden and finds himself alone there with a dog with very big teeth. The dog, for the moment, shows no signs of aggressiveness. The best thing for us to do is surely to try to establish, as between the two of us, the assumption that teeth have nothing whatsoever to do with our mutual relationship—that they are neither here nor there. If the dog shows no disposition to assume that it is otherwise, why should we raise

the subject and invite attention to the disparity?": *Memoirs, 1925–50*, vol. 1 (Boston: Little, Brown, 1967), p. 408. See also James Forrestal's views in *Foreign Relations of the United States, 1948*, vol. 1, part 2, *General; The United Nations* (Washington, D.C.: Government Printing Office, 1976), p. 542. For a related discussion see George Quester, "Defining Strategic Issues: How to Avoid Isometric Exercises," in Robert Harkavy and Edward Kolodziej, eds., *American Security Policy and Policy-Making* (Lexington, Mass.: Lexington Books, 1980), pp. 195–207.

22. Richard Ned Lebow, *Between Peace and War: The Nature of International Crisis* (Baltimore: Johns Hopkins University Press, 1981); Lebow, "Clear and Future Danger: Managing Relations with the Soviet Union in the 1980s," in Robert O'Neill and D. Horner, eds., *New Directions in Strategic Thinking* (London: Allen & Unwin, 1981), pp. 221–45. Secretary Brown notes the dangers posed by the Soviet Union's becoming desperate, but does not consider how U.S. policy might reduce or inadvertently contribute to this (DoD, *Annual Report, F.Y. 1980*, pp. 4, 18, 38, 60).

23. John Steinbruner, "Launch under Attack," *Scientific American*, 250 (January 1984), 37–47.

24. Thomas Schelling, *Strategy of Conflict* (Cambridge: Harvard University Press, 1960), pp. 43–46.

25. John Erickson, "The Soviet View of Deterrence: A General Survey," *Survival*, 24 (November/December 1982), 244. George Kennan also has pointed to the danger that American policies will lead the Soviet Union to conclude that war is inevitable: *The Nuclear Delusion* (New York: Pantheon, 1983), pp. xxvi–xxvii, 102, 235. In this context, it should be noted that the problem with the Pershing II and the Trident II is not that they would force the Russians to put their missiles on launch-on-warning status, but that the Russians might fear that they would not get enough warning to be able to launch their missiles before these American forces landed and so might feel great pressures to strike preemptively.

26. The point that whether deterrence succeeds or fails can depend in part on what the other side thinks the outcome of negotiations will probably be is made by Janice Stein, "Calculation, Miscalculation, and Conventional Deterrence: The View from Cairo," in Jervis, Lebow, and Stein, *Psychology and Deterrence*; Richard Ned Lebow, "Miscalculation in the South Atlantic: The Origins of the Falkland War," *Journal of Strategic Studies*, 6 (March 1983), 10; and Warren Cohen, "The United States and China since 1945," in Cohen, ed. *New Frontiers in American-East Asian Relations* (New York: Columbia University Press, 1983), pp. 154–55. For a discussion of Soviet behavior in these terms, see Dennis Ross, "Risk Aversion in Soviet Decision-Making," in Jiri Valenta and William Potter, eds., *Soviet National Security Decision-Making* (London: Allen & Unwin, 1984).

27. See, for example, John Rose, *The Evolution of U.S. Army Nuclear Doctrine: 1945–1980* (Boulder, Colo.: Westview Press, 1980), p. 170; U.S. Senate, Committee on Armed Services, *Modernization of the U.S. Strategic Deterrent*, 97th Cong., 1st sess. (Washington, D.C. Government Printing Office, 1982), p. 58.

One of the earliest academic discussions of this strategy is Klaus Knorr and Thornton Read, eds., *Limited Strategic War* (New York: Praeger, 1962).

28. This point is missed by many analysts who deny that nuclear weapons have any utility save for protection of a state's homeland. It is also missed by some of the critics of the limited use of nuclear weapons, who see the potential for explosive escalation as so great as to rule out any use of the tactics discussed here. See, for example, Hans Morgenthau, "The Four Paradoxes of Nuclear Strategy," *American Political Science Review*, 58 (March 1964), 23–35.

29. Since the question of whether to put forces on alert is a political as well as a military one, analysts must not restrict their attention to the sorts of warnings about Soviet activity which could be expected, but must also consider what American decision-makers would be willing to do on the basis of that information. See George and Smoke, *Deterrence in American Foreign Policy*, pp. 367–87 and Richard Betts, *Surprise Attack* (Washington, D.C.: Brookings Institution, 1982).

30. George and Smoke, *Deterrence in American Foreign Policy*, pp. 536–40. Also see Smoke, *War: Controlling Escalation* (Cambridge: Harvard University Press, 1977), and Pierre Gallois, *The Balance of Terror* (Boston: Houghton Mifflin, 1961). Dean Acheson's initial approach to the defense of Europe seems to have been based on similar reasoning: NATO must be able to block "the technique of the *fait accompli*. . . . It is the aim of this program to insure that a successful swift and comparatively effortless military action by an aggressor would be impossible and therefore to make the gamble too hazardous to be tempting": *Department of State Bulletin*, 21 (August 8, 1949), 193.

31. See, for example, John Mearsheimer, "Why the Soviets Can't Win Quickly in Central Europe," *International Security*, 7 (Summer 1982), 3–39. Although many analysts say that Russian doctrine is based on a blitzkrieg, John Erickson disagrees, arguing that the Soviets feel that this tactic is too risky: "The Soviet View of Deterrence," pp. 246–47.

32. U.S. House of Representatives, Subcommittee on International Security and International Affairs of the Committee on Foreign Affairs, *Overview of Nuclear Arms Control and Defense Strategy in NATO*, 97th Cong., 2d sess. (Washington, D.C.: Government Printing Office, 1982), p. 210. Also see Harold Brown, *Thinking about National Security* (Boulder, Colo.: Westview, 1983), p. 102. But since Brown presents no argument as to why this capability is important, one cannot tell whether his reasoning is the same as that presented here.

33. Kenneth Waltz, "A Strategy for the Rapid Deployment Force," *International Security*, 5 (Spring 1981), 49–73.

34. Clausewitz, *On War*, ed. and trans. Michael Howard and Peter Paret (Princeton: Princeton University Press, 1976), p. 75.

Index

Index

Library of Congress Cataloging in Publication Data

Jervis, Robert, 1940–
   The illogic of American nuclear strategy.

   (Cornell studies in security affairs)
   Includes index.
   1. United States—Military policy. 2. Atomic weapons. 3. Strategy. I. Title.
II. Series.
UA23.J47   1984   355'.0217'0973   84-7731
ISBN 0-8014-1715-5 (alk. paper)